Heaven is real and FUN

You don't float around wearing diapers and eating grapes!

Heaven as seen by
KIM ROBINSON

Heaven is Real and Fun

Copyright © 2016 by Kim Robinson
Revised 2020
Edited by Dorothea LeBlanc in 2023

Heaven is Real and Fun
by Kim Robinson

Printed in the United States of America.

All rights reserved solely by the author. The author guarantees all contents are original and do not infringe upon the legal rights of any other person or work. No part of this book may be reproduced in any form without the permission of the author. The views expressed in this book are not necessarily those of the publisher.

Unless otherwise indicated, Scripture quotations taken from the Amplified Bible (AMP). Copyright © 1954, 1958, 1962, 1964, 1965, 1987 by The Lockman Foundation. Used by permission. All rights reserved.

Quote from Bobby Conner Shepherd's Rod Volume XIX 2014

Heaven is Real and Fun

Table of Contents

Acknowledgments xii
Endorsements xv
Introduction xix

Chapter 1
Playing with Jesus 23

1988–1997
My Mansion 23
Rollercoaster 28
Play Gel Balls 29
The Body Parts Storehouse 31
The Children 34
The Flying Game 37
House of Laughter 38
Jesus Is in Me 40

2001–2010
The Money Room 42
Jesus Is My Shepherd 46
Let's Fly with Jesus 47

Heaven Is Real and I'm Coming Back 48
Light Heals 49
Eyes to See 49
Rose Petals Falling 51

2011

Fragrance of Jesus 52
Thick Gel 52
Snow Sledding with Jesus 53
Tree House/Slide with Jesus 55
Lying with Jesus 55
Floating in the River 57
Body Surfing 59
Jump; JUST JUMP 59
Jump, Jump 60
Don't Be Afraid of the Future 61
Jesus Is Fun 61
Expensive Perfume 63
Whirlwind 64
Water Volcano 64
Jesus Does the Cha-Cha 65
Flower Petals 65
Dancing around His Throne 65
Precious Jewels 65

2012

Walk through Pictures 66
Jesus in a Bar 67
The High Praise Room/Blue Crystals 68

Table of Contents

Doing Nothing with Jesus 69
Cloud of Witnesses Say, "Go-Go-Go" 70
Gondola Boat Ride with Jesus 71
Daddy and Mama Are Solid/Park and Swings 71
Jesus' Courtyard 73
Wrapped in His Presence 73
Be Content 74
It Doesn't Matter 75
Hammock Chair 76
Peace of Mind in My Rock House 77
Playing in the Snow with Jesus 78
Fuzzy Slippers Appear 79

2013

Spoiled Child 80
Swinging in a Jungle 80
Dancing and Cooking with Jesus 81
Jesus' Garden 82
Jesus' Blue Room 83
Relationship Makes the Fruit 84
Jesus Dunked Me 84
The Scroll 84
Hidden in Him 85
Leap Time and Space 86
I Can Smell Him 87

2014–2015

Swimming with Jesus 88
Lots of Bubbles 89

Breathe in Life 90

Jesus' Ice Skates 91

Chapter 2
Daddy God and the Holy Spirit in Heaven 93

2000–2011

Storehouse of Elements 95

God's Not Good; He's Magnificent 98

Ascending Is a Tool 99

My Father Is an Artist 100

Petals of Favor 101

I Would Look over the Edge 102

Let It Go 103

The Light Room 104

God's Fog Machine 105

God Loves the Smell of Worship 106

Holy Spirit Baton 106

2012

Daddy Smells Like Love, Openness, and Rain 107

Daddy Said, "I Know All" 108

Flying Around the Throne 109

Waterfall Swing 110

I Saw the Holy Spirit 111

2013

God's Rose Garden 112

Clover Crown 114

Table of Contents

Mud Castles with Daddy God 114
Tunnel under the Throne 115
Holy Spirit has Light Hair 116
Holy Spirit Loves the ER 116
You Heard Their Cries 117
Blue Flower Canopy 118
Daddy Whittles 119
Soft, Fuzzy Animals 120
I've Got You 121
Daddy's So Nice 122

2014
Daddy God's Hair 123
Daddy God Turned Transparent 124
See, Follow, Hear, Follow with Your Heart 125
Enlarge My Spirit 126

Chapter 3
Animals and Angels in Heaven 129

2009–2011
Butterflies 129
Pets in Heaven 130
I'm in the Army of the Lord 131
Riding in Darkness 134
Riding a Huge Eagle 135
Talk to the Animals 136
Angel Named Entertaining 137
Riding a Horse in Heaven 140

2012–2014

Fighting on a Horse 141
Riding a Lion in the Blood 142
Angel and His Robe 143
Angel Named Tom 144
Flying on an Eagle 144
Angels Replaced What Was Missing 145
Dancing Fairy 146
Mermaid-Type Water Angel 146
Bridegroom's Chamber and Angel Erin 146
Butterfly Angels Worship 148
Angel Called Prosperity 149
Fun House 149

Chapter 4
People and Other Fun Events 151

1995–2000

Meeting Daniel, Joshua, Moses, Noah, Ruth, and David 151
Translated to Arabia, Turkey, and China 155
Popping Bones 156
The Changing Room 156

2011

You'll Never Ride Alone 157
Translated to Los Angeles, California 158
Translated to Hawaii 158
Snowy Mountain 159

2012–2014
They Pray for You! 160
Britain 161
Table in Heaven 161
They Want to Teach You, People in White 162
White Round Light 162

Conclusion 163

"I have made you known to them, and will continue to make you known in order that the love you have for me may be in them and that I myself may be in them." John 17:26

Acknowledgments

I would really like to thank my personal editors Wayne and his wife Sandra. Thanks also to Billie, Cathy, Deborah, Laura, my sweet family, and friends for all your advice, time, and patience.

Picture Acknowledgments

Pam Finlay (you may purchase a color print from www.crystalclearcreations.com.au):

Riding on His Covenant Promises
Leaning on the Beloved
Freedom

Brightlights Photography in Rogers, Arkansas:

Snowy Mountain
Harvest
Running Water
Walk
Running Stream
Swing
Be Content

Ice
Mia
Horse in Yellow Flowers
Deer
Jerry and Kim Robinson

ABS Website:

Roller Coaster
Joy
Falling Flower Petals
Just Jump
Waterfall
Log House
Yellow Butterfly and Flower
Bright Butterfly
Flying Eagle
Fighting Horse
Lion
Eagle Head
Fireplace

Lighting Photo by C. Edward Houston, Rogers, Arkansas

Endorsements

Kim is a friend and confidant. She is a wife, mom, and grandma. She is a mentor and a "mom" to many young women. She is also a backyard chicken-raising enthusiast; I have enjoyed hearing her stories as she adopted the chicks, constructed a coop, and cared for her birds through the wintery cold and summer heat.

I first met Kim through a local House of Prayer as we served together in Sozo Ministry. Kim carries a joy and enthusiasm that is contagious—the natural fruit of her relationship with her Daddy God. She lives her life in close proximity to Daddy God, walking a consistent walk of childlike faith and simplicity. She is open and real, someone you immediately feel comfortable with.

Since 1988 the Lord, or I should say Daddy God, has allowed Kim to see and experience Heaven—to see, hear, feel, and even taste the reality and fun of Heaven. From time to time Kim would share these experiences with her close friends. But over the past year Daddy God has prompted her to share her experiences with a larger audience in writing with you and me. What a blessing! We Christians tend to get bogged down on earth, and we lose our perspective and wonder of God and Heaven. There is an encouraging message in this book for each of us to not lose our wonder and childlikeness with regard to Jesus and Heaven. It's real—Jesus is real—and it is fun! I am excited about this book because it will bring encouragement to you and me. Yes, it may also stretch and challenge us and our way of thinking. I am thankful for Kim's obedience to share what she has been shown. I believe she is stewarding a gift she has received. My prayer is that we would be given a renewed and fresh wonder of Heaven (the eternal home that Jesus has made ready for us), and that we would carry that mindset with us here in our daily lives.

Dawn Roach
Sozo Gateway Team Administrator

In a time when the world is full of doubt and confusion about eternal life, a story emerges that will spark conversation and expectation of what life in Heaven will be like. The thing that makes God so amazing is how each individual has their own story to tell, and this is Kim Robinson's story. How her journey with God led her to supernatural encounters that changed her view of God and of our eternal life with Jesus. Our individual experiences are not to create biblical doctrine but to ignite our passion to seek Jesus and know Him. This journey will challenge you and inspire you to seek a real relationship with a loving Savior. As you read Kim's story, keep your eyes on Jesus and let Him open your heart to an awesome God.

Pastor Josh Davis
Life Connection Church

In a time when so many are asking: "If Heaven is for real … ," Kim brings a bird's eye view of her experiences in Heaven. This book is uplifting, encouraging, and hopeful. I would also say that it will bring some surprise to your heart as to all that goes on in Heaven while we, here on earth, are experiencing life. I have known Kim for twenty-five years, and we have

Endorsements

traveled many places together. I know her heart, and I know her life. So sit back and get ready to share in Kim's adventures in Heaven.

Mary Haynes
Director of Joppa House of Prayer

Kim Robinson has been one to inspire me in my walk as a believer. Within her walk with God and the encounters she receives is a personification of what we too could experience in our lives for simply being children of God; we are deeply loved and accepted. She neither boasts nor claims to be a saint. However, she does admit to walk with Him in a way like a little child would approach her daddy in the natural realm. Because of this and the simple joy she carries, Kim has experienced the beauty and simplicity of what Heaven is like in a fun way. She is one of the many catalysts who has impacted and will continue to impact people who have doubted the authenticity of Heaven and maybe Jesus himself. When we read and immerse ourselves in her real-life journeys, I believe Kim's experiences will awaken our hearts for more of God, to draw closer to Him and steer our burning hearts to experience a greater adventure beyond what we see in the physical. At the end of the day, Kim's heart is to express this vast, beautiful love that God has for us and to share what is possible if we too choose to spend time in His presence. Sharing her secret-place journey with the world, she hopes to encourage us in our Christian walk to seek more and go beyond what we already know. So, open the door; open this beautiful golden gate vested with jewels and be mesmerized not only by the truth of His promises, but by Jesus himself. Heaven is real and . . fun.

Janina Thompson
Missionary to Thailand

Heaven is Real and Fun

Introduction

The Holy Spirit has been taking me to Heaven since 1988. This began not long after I had given my life to Jesus and I had made Him my Lord.

In Heaven, I would meet Jesus and He would show me various fun places. We would do fun things together and He let me participate in many events. On one visit I asked Daddy God, "Why are You showing me these places?" And He said,

> "Because people think all they do here is float around wearing diapers, eating grapes, or doing nothing but bowing before Me.
>
> It's like someone is planning a party and the person you are planning the party for really thinks it's going to be boring so they don't want to come.
>
> It saddens Me that my children don't want to come here. I have planned for each person, in detail, an eternity that will make them happy to be here with Me. So you are to tell them, 'Heaven is real and fun, and Jesus is coming soon!'"

This book is about the heart of the Father, about His love for you and your love for Him. You may not have known this closeness was possible with the God of Heaven—who is your Father, your Daddy, your Abba, your Papa—but He wants you to know Him!

And so this fun intimacy that I have with Jesus is also available for you, if you have asked Jesus Christ to be the Lord and Savior of your life.

It's time for us to slow down, unplug, turn off, come away, and spend time developing a relationship with the One we're going to spend eternity with. I want to give you a quote from Bobby Conners' Shepherd's Rod Volume XIX, 2014.

> "God's people are being ushered into an intimacy beyond anything we have ever experienced. We're maturing into a heart-based and Spirit-led relationship with our Lord Jesus Christ and our Father, not out of a relationship based on "mental assent" and mere "head knowledge." This intimacy is based on revelation—not carnal information. He goes on to say, "God is revealing how to walk on the pathway to victory and live above the chaos and confusion of the 'spirit of this age' and culture."

You are not weird, strange, or crazy if you really want to experience, or have already experienced, or are just beginning to experience encounters like I am sharing with you in this book. I share them only to encourage you in your relationship with Jesus, Holy Spirit, and Daddy God.

In this book, I have listed the time I spent with Jesus first because that's who I met first in the spirit realm. As I began to trust Him, He took me to the Father. It is all about trusting in God and His great love for you.

Introduction

By the way, you may not find all of the events described in this book in the Bible, but you will find they do not contradict the Bible, God's character, God's nature, or His love for you.

This is my story; this is my journey about Heaven.
Mrs. Kim Robinson

Heaven is Real and Fun

Chapter 1

Playing with Jesus

1988–1997

My Mansion

After laying the girls down for a nap upstairs, I went downstairs (in my log house) and sat on the floor in the laundry room. That was the place I would go to spend quiet time and worship Jesus. I turned on some worship music and sang where I knew no one could see or hear me. Then after a bit, I turned on softer, soaking-type worship music.

"Soaking" may be a new term for some; soaking is really about resting in the Lord and learning to be still. Sometimes the voice of the Lord is a whisper—a still, small voice.

If you are going through times when it feels like you cannot hear the voice of the Lord, it may mean you are too busy or you are too loud. It may mean your circumstances are too loud. Soaking is a way of learning to be still and practicing to be God-conscious. In that stillness, God can speak with words, pictures, or feelings. When you make that time available by

Heaven is Real and Fun

---

sitting or lying on the floor (or whatever it is you do to be still), He will show up and speak.

So, I was worshiping the Lord quietly for about one hour when I felt my spirit go up. Even though my body was sitting down, I knew my spirit was going up; it felt like a layer of my spirit ascended.

Suddenly I was standing, as maybe a 25 year old, in what seemed to be an open field. Jesus was standing there and He began to walk over to me. He put His arms around me and gave me a big hug. I didn't know what to do so I just stood there thinking, "Oh my God, Jesus is hugging me. What do I do?"

He took my hand and said, "Come, walk with me."

Well, I had never walked in Heaven before. I didn't even know how to walk in Heaven so I just stood there as He began to walk ahead, holding onto my hand. Instantly He knew my dilemma, though I hadn't said anything. So Jesus stepped back to my side and while still holding my hand, He looked down at my feet.

He said, "Pick up your left foot." I lifted up my left foot, and not knowing what to do next, I just kept it there.

He said, "Now put it down," so I stretched it out and put it down. Then He said, "Now lift up your right foot."

I thought, "Oh, here we go, we are going to fly off like Peter Pan!" But nothing happened.

Jesus said, "Now put it down," so I stretched it out and put it down.

Jesus patiently said, "Now pick up your left foot." So I lifted it up slowly stretching it out, and I put it down.

Then with the most embarrassing gasp I thought, "Oh no, you just *walk*!!" I was totally embarrassed that the first time I met Jesus, I did something so silly! Jesus laughed at my thought.

It was then that I realized He could hear my thoughts! Oh no, I thought to myself, "Blank thoughts, blank thoughts, blank thoughts!" And Jesus laughed again!

I thought, "Oh well, I can't do this all the time," so I just relaxed.

As we began to walk, holding hands, the embarrassment subsided and I could see from a distance the tops of palaces. I had a knowing these were mansions that Jesus had created for each one of us who love Him. Some had shiny pointed bright gold tops, and some had shiny round decorated tops such as those you would see in other countries, like maybe Russia. Some were taller than others and some were wider than others, but they were all different.

Jesus asked, "Would you like to see your mansion?"

I said, "Yes!" We walked slowly up a slight hill. I was walking barefoot and noticed we were walking in dirt. It was the softest dirt I had ever felt; it felt like baby powder but was tan-colored like dirt. One of the neat things is when I lifted up my foot, the dirt would fall right off, so my feet never got dirty.

When we walked up to the front door of my mansion, Jesus with His right hand reached over and opened the tall oval door and stood to the side. I thought, "Oh that's just like Jesus, to be a gentleman." I stepped inside and went down two steps.

I was excited to have a sunken living room. And the floor was amazing to say the least! I had never seen a marble floor, but my floor was made of the most beautiful marble. I could tell that it was about two to three *feet* thick. I looked up to where Jesus was standing; He was just inside the door watching me and smiling.

Then I saw one of the walls that was about fifteen feet high, it had "gold" swirls like wood grain except the swirls were real, thick gold. I had a knowing that this gold wasn't inlaid—the whole wall, gold and all, was just supernaturally made like this. Where there would normally be knotholes, like in wood grain paneling, there were huge diamonds, rubies, emeralds, yellow stones, and other precious stones of all colors. I don't know what kind they were, but they were about the size of a huge orange or a small grapefruit. The wall was so natural looking, the stones did not appear to have been inserted either, they were just part of the wall material.

I stood there with my mouth open, breathless at the beauty of just this one wall! I looked at Jesus standing there and He laughed; not at me because Jesus wouldn't laugh at me. He was laughing because I was so amazed at what He had planned for me. I could see that He was happy that I was happy!

He said, "Whatever you have to go through on earth, it's worth it all. For you're only there for a short time. But you're here in Heaven, at home, for eternity! Do you want to see more?"

"Yes," I said.

We walked into a room that had a huge bed. I thought, "Why would there be a bed, how could anyone be sleepy or tired here?"

Jesus, knowing my thoughts said, "Where do you like to talk?" Oh right, I could see my kids and me lying across the bed, laughing and talking. I could see my sisters and me lying across the bed, laughing and talking. And I could see my friends and me doing the same.

Jesus said, "It's a comfortable, cozy place to laugh and talk, a more intimate place to relax."

Then I spotted this bright beautiful flowering plant growing on the wall. Jesus said, "Break it apart and put it anywhere you want to." I broke off a piece of the flowering plant and held it against the wall. There was so much life in the wall that the piece instantly grew roots, attached itself, and began to grow. I did it again, and that piece of the flowering plant also instantly began to grow.

Jesus said, "There's so much life here, even in the walls!"

There was also an archway-type door in the living room that I didn't go through. I felt like it was connected to something huge, perhaps to other mansions or to the rest of mine. The best way to describe the feeling is like the feeling you have in a huge hotel where everyone has their own place but yet you're all still connected.

Jesus is excited about what He has made for you, and He wants you to be excited about it too. This event reminds me of the scripture that tells about the Father's house.

> Let not your heart be troubled: ye believe in God, believe also in me. In my Father's house are many mansions: if it were not so, I would have told you. I go to prepare a place for you. And if I go and prepare a place for you, I will come again, and receive you unto myself; that where I am, there ye may be also. (John 14:1–3 KJV)

Rollercoaster

I was worshiping when I heard Jesus say, "Come here and stand up so you can see!" I didn't know how to "come up" but then I saw a hand with a white sleeve reach down to me. I reached up, and instantly I was standing at an amusement park with games, rides, and animals. I saw Jesus and we hugged. Again, I found myself to be a young looking adult. He took me by the hand and as we walked around I could feel the excitement in the air. This amusement park was clean, and laughter filled the air. There were lots of games to play and prizes to be won. People and families were walking together carrying very large stuffed toys, laughing, and holding hands.

Everything was free because Jesus has paid the price.

We walked up to ride a rollercoaster and I noticed we were the first ones in line. Looking around I realized we would always be the first in line; that's the way it was at this park. There were no waiting lines even though many people were riding rides, playing games, and petting the animals.

There was a high set of stairs before me, and as I looked up, we were instantly at the top of the stairs. As we got in the ride and sat down, pulling the handle closed, I noticed there wasn't a tight-fitting seat belt on the rollercoaster. I was a little afraid because the ride was huge with lots of loops and drops. Jesus, sitting next to me with His brown hair and beautiful smile, reached over with a loving look in His eyes and put His hand on my hands as I gripped the handle.

He said, "I would never make something that would hurt you!" Knowing that I could ride this and not get hurt, sick, or stuck upside down caused me to relax, and I was ready to go.

The ride began to roll forward; the excitement and anticipation of the thrill was overwhelming! It soon made huge loops and gigantic drops. When we made a loop up and would come back down, the tracks would spread so we could go through them, and then they would go back together again (that's something I don't think has ever been made on earth). We would make a huge drop and climb back up for a loop to the left and then to the right just before another huge drop. I don't even think a rollercoaster on earth could be made tall enough to accomplish so many of these long drops.

As we rolled into the station to get off, Jesus looked at me and asked, "Did you like that?"

He knew I loved it and that I wanted to go again, so we were instantly at the top of the stairs, next in line to get on for another ride! I could ride this roller coaster as many times as I wanted. The seat was soft and conformed to my body and the temperature was perfect. It was so exciting and overwhelmingly fun!

Play Gel Balls

This morning while worshiping, I was caught up in the spirit and stepped over into Heaven (as an adult) when I heard Jesus say, "Come play gel balls!"

These gel balls are squishy like a water balloon but are full of giggly joy-gel, and you can even squeeze them into yourself! When you put one into yourself, you start to laugh intensely! (In the spirit realm you can place things into yourself as if you were a transparent pocket.)

Jesus started to throw these gel balls at me and I laughed! He threw them at other people who were also throwing them at other people (children were there too). It was a lot like a large game of dodgeball except when you try to hit another person with these joy-gel balls, instead of running away they would actually run and *try* to get hit so the gel would go into them, and make them really laugh hard. Or sometimes, they would catch a gel ball, squeeze it into themselves, have a big giggly laugh and then continue playing.

Heaven is so fun and filled with extreme joy! This reminded me of Job 8:21 that says,

> He will yet fill your mouth with laughter and your lips with joyful shouting.

Another time while I was praying at home, Jesus said, "Today isn't a work day but a fun day. Let's play!"

I went with Jesus and He showed me different balls that were filled with gel and they were falling down around us! He said, "When these balls hit you they fill you with life. The liquid inside of these gels balls is filled with life."

It was raining gel balls and so I ran through them like a child with my arms stretched out, laughing and trying to get hit, but also trying to dodge them at the same time. When a ball hit me the gel went in and through me. I was so full of life and energy and had an effect like electricity would recharge a battery. They looked like the colored balls from McDonald's or Chucky Cheese, or like large paint balls—but not filled with paint, and they don't hurt. They were just big balls filled with liquid life.

The Body Parts Storehouse

I had been praising, singing, dancing, and worshiping Jesus, and then I quieted myself and focused on Jesus' face. I felt myself walk through into the spirit. Jesus met me and we hugged. I again appeared as an adult.

He said, "I want to show you something!" Suddenly I was standing on what seemed to be clouds. We walked into a clean white room that had many individual legs hanging from up above. They were over a rail like clothes hanging over a railing. They were perfect, they had a knee cap, an ankle, a foot with toes, and flawlessly smooth skin.

Then I saw spines hanging over a rail with the soft thick cartilage between the joints. They had the typical neck curvature all the way down to the tailbone—perfectly formed to the very tip. There were all different sizes, from infant to adult.

Then I saw perfectly formed, healthy lungs of all sizes in open trays. I thought, "Don't these need some sort of plastic wrap like "Press n Seal" or "Saran Wrap"?

Jesus laughed, "In Heaven, there is no need to keep bacteria out because there isn't bacteria in Heaven."

I saw various colors of eyes in jars without lids. One jar would have all blue eyes, one would have all brown, one hazel, one green, and so forth. You know, there are different shades of blues and browns, greens, and hazel so there were many many different jars for all the different colors. The pupils of the eyes were perfect, the colors were bright, and even the whites of the eyes were clear and a very pretty white.

As we walked on, Jesus said, "People whose backs have been seriously burned are going to receive new skin, and people whose faces have been burned are going to receive soft baby-smooth skin." I also knew anyone who had ANY type of skin problem was also in this category.

I saw jars full of sperm on one wall and women's eggs in jars on the other wall—rows and rows of them.

Jesus said, "There are people who are barren because they don't know how to claim "these". So they need to find my promises and stand on them. They cry and plead and beg me for a child. They will adopt, or foster, or volunteer at a school to prove to me what a good parent they would be. They cry out to me to give them children, when all along their children are here! All they have to do is find my promise and stand on it, and they will come!"

I have added a few promise scriptures here for you to stand on. Take time to read and meditate on them.

Legs

I will walk before the Lord in the land of the living. (Psalm 116:9)

The blind receive their sight and the lame walk, lepers are cleansed (by healing) and the deaf hear, the dead are raised up and the poor have good news (the Gospel) preached to them. (Matthew 11:5)

Eyes

The Lord opens the eyes of the blind, the Lord lifts up those who are bowed down, the Lord loves the [uncompromisingly] righteous (those upright in heart and in right standing with Him). (Psalm 146:8)

Lungs

Thus says God the Lord—He Who created the Heavens and stretched them forth, He Who spread abroad the earth and that which comes out of it, He Who gives breath to the people on it and spirit to those who walk in it. (Isaiah 42:5)

Skin

Then [God] is gracious to him and says, Deliver him from going down into the pit [of destruction]; I have found a ransom (a price of redemption, an atonement)!

[Then the man's] flesh shall be restored; it becomes fresher and more tender than a child's; he returns to the days of his youth. (Job 33:24–25)

Sperm and Eggs

Is anything too hard or too wonderful for the Lord? (Genesis 18:14)

For You did form my inward parts; You did knit me together in my mother's womb. (Psalm 139:13)

Now FAITH is the assurance (the confirmation, the title deed) of the things (we) hope for, being the proof of things (we) do NOT SEE and the conviction of their reality (faith perceiving as real fact what is not revealed to the senses)! (Hebrews 11:1)

The Children

After we came out of the Body Parts Storehouse Jesus said, "Do you want to see something else?"

I thought, "Man, what could beat seeing legs hanging from the rafters?" But I said, "Yes!"

Jesus replied, "Let's walk over here," and we walked up a path toward a building.

He said, "Are you ready? Can you handle this?"

Again I thought, "Hey, I just handled living body parts hanging from a railing and real eyeballs looking at me," so excitedly I said, "Yes!"

Jesus and I approached this large white building that had a smooth texture on the outside (like pearl or marble). There was a very big white oval-shaped door that appeared to be made of exotic wood or ivory, and it was carved with lots of detail. Jesus opened the door.

Some children who appeared to be around six to ten years old came running out to see Jesus. Two or three of the children ran up to Jesus and wrapped their arms around Him, laughing and so happy to see Him.

I thought, "That's how the little children love Jesus in the Bible!"

One little red-headed girl ran up to me, wrapped her arms around me and looked up at me with a great big smile and so much love! I looked at her and thought, "Ahh, she's so sweet and loving to me. How nice!" And then the children turned and ran back inside the room.

Jesus and I walked up to the door and stood at the opening, Sometimes when a person just stands at a door but doesn't go in, they can only see a little to the left and to the right. From where I was, I could see about a hundred children, ranging from crawling age on one side of the room to about twelve years old on the other side.

The children were involved in a very loud, but fun and happy activity. Across the brightly lit room there was a lady who resembled a nun standing in the back. She appeared to be wearing a habit and veil, and was cheerfully watching all the children play.

I thought, "Well, of course a nun would be watching over the children in Heaven because that's what they like to do on the earth; they enjoy kids so much!"

It must have been recess time or something because I noticed the children were playing with a huge, brightly colored beach ball. They were so happy playing and laughing with each other, jumping with strong legs and hitting the ball with strong arms up in the air from one end of the room to the other. Obviously, it's Heaven, and no one was getting hurt.

I asked Jesus, "What is this place?"

Jesus said, "These are the children who have been aborted. They are being raised here with Me."

I thought, "They know *why* they are here! I bet they have so much hatred for their moms and dads, and for the doctors and nurses, and for everyone else involved."

Jesus turned and looked at me and said, "No. They don't have any hatred for them. They love them all! They know who was really behind it. They know the devil was the one who caused the lust and inspired the actions. They don't hate anyone. Love is what they do. They love their parents and are not mad at anyone."

Then Jesus slowly closed the door. I could see that He was feeling really sad. I watched as He walked over to a tree stump and sat down. He began to cry—a deep heavy cry from the heart.

I was suddenly aware of a very, very tall man standing beside me. It was an angel and I asked Him, "Why is Jesus crying like that?" The angel said, "Another one just arrived."

Later that day while I was praying in my home, I saw Jesus standing in front of me in a vision. I asked Him, "Why were you sitting on a tree stump? Why wasn't it a golden throne or chair?"

He said, "What does a stump represent? It is something that began to grow but was cut off."

He also told me at that time, that the little red-haired girl who hugged me was mine! You see, I'd had an abortion at nineteen. It never dawned on me that the little red-headed girl could possibly be mine until Jesus told me. All I knew was that she looked up at me with such love. I didn't know who she was, but she knew who I was!

I have named her Joy because she is very much alive, full of joy, and she loves me. She has known nothing but Heaven, with no shame, guilt, or hatred.

Matthew 18:11 says, "It is not the will of the Father that one should be lost."

Flying Game

I had just lain my girls down for the night, and after putting our miniature sheltie dog out and cleaning up the kitchen, I headed for the downstairs utility room to pray. Closing the door quietly behind me, putting on my favorite worship music while standing, I began to worship Jesus… and He said to me, "I want to show you Heaven."

Suddenly, we were standing on a high mountain cliff looking straight down when He said, "Now jump!" (I was about as old as a teenager.)

Trusting Jesus and holding His hand, side by side we jumped! But we didn't fall—we flew! We flew up and down, and it seemed we were controlling where we went with our thoughts, but we also used our arms to turn. Once I was confident that I wouldn't fall, Jesus let go of me so I could fly by myself.

There were rollercoaster-type hills that we could fly over and loop around and fly straight down, going extremely fast. There were air tunnels where the turbulence was so strong we would be tossed and turned and rolled around. I wasn't scared, hurt, confused, or sick but I did laugh so intensely. It was really fun!

While we were flying, there were games with objects we'd have to follow along, objects like a steep hill or a really sharp turn. Signs would pop up in front of us and we'd have to be quick to turn left or right or maybe up or down. These signs that gave us instructions reminded me of the children's game "Simon Says".

One sign might read, "Do a double summersault," so I would do it and then keep flying extremely fast on the trail. Another sign would pop up and read, "Do a swan dive," so I would do a quick swan dive.

When we were done, Jesus and I laughed and hugged because it was so exhilarating, challenging, and fun.

Jesus asked, "Did you like that?"

I said, "Oh man, let's do it again!" And instantly we were back at the beginning of the game, always first in line.

House of Laughter

I had just finished mowing the back yard after taking my girls to school when I headed downstairs to my prayer room to spend some intimate time worshiping Jesus. Turning on my favorite praise music and reading a few scriptures to get my mind quieted down and focused, I began to worship and instantly I was in Heaven.

Jesus, an angel, and I all went to a place called 'The House of Laughter." We walked across this extremely long swinging bridge high up in the air. Then we walked through a door and entered a room. The angel stayed back

Playing with Jesus

---

at the door as Jesus and I went in to play. I was a young adult in my 20's or maybe my teens.

The floor shook with a million tiny little shakes and made our faces and bodies tingle as they vibrated. I tried to walk but ended up crawling; I was really laughing hard the whole time, and could hear loud laughter coming from the other rooms.

Then I crawled across an ice maze, but I didn't get wet or cold. It was just super slick. The slippery floor was made of different sized ice cubes that rotated. I couldn't hang onto the bigger ones because they would slip out of my arms. Jesus and I would slip, slide, and roll around bumping into the large ice cubes and each other, laughing and laughing.

As I went to the next room, I was able to stand up and enjoy watching the funniest videos of people and even me, as children, doing things that were hilarious. In Heaven there is no heaviness or worry, so it's very easy to laugh.

Next there was a slide that Jesus and I took a ride on. We slid down and looped around and shot out into a huge room that was weightless. People were floating around and laughing because there were suction holes of various sizes along the wall that vibrated.

Looking around, I saw people who had part of a leg or the side of their head, their back, cheek, stomach, or rear end sucked into one of the small vibrating holes. When someone managed to pull themselves off (and it was difficult because they'd be laughing so hard they'd barely have any strength left), they'd get sucked over to another vibrating hole.

There was a small door up high that we were trying to get to. Once we got free and floated upward, we could go through that upper door and slide down and around to the front door to go again if we wanted. Jesus, and I landed in a heap, piled on top of each other laughing so much that it was hard to stand up to walk.

Jesus wants you to come know Him personally and to enjoy being with Him:

> And [that you may come] to know [practically, through personal experience] the love of Christ which far surpasses [mere] knowledge [without experience], that you may be filled up [throughout your being] to all the fullness of God [so that you may have the richest experience of God's presence in your lives, completely filled and flooded with God Himself]. (Ephesians 3:19)

Jesus Is in Me

I had just gotten back from my morning jog. After cooling down and getting a big glass of ice water I headed downstairs to my prayer room, the utility room. Sitting down on a small rug on the cement floor in front of the washer and dryer, I began reading some scriptures in Revelation 5 to get my mind focused and quieted down. I began to worship Jesus.

I felt His presence come into the room and instantly I was with Jesus, standing by an ocean. I appeared there as an adult (21-25 years old), and as we walked together He put His arm around me, patted my hands and said, "You know, I've given you gifts."

I said, "I know." Haha, but I'm guessing I *didn't* know or He wouldn't have told me. He leaned His head over on mine as we walked. Then stopping, He turned to me so we were face to face.

He said, "You know I'm in you," and He just walked straight into me!! I could feel Him pass through me.

He said, "I'm beside you," and He walked out my right side with His left arm still inside my right arm. I felt a tingling feeling as He stood facing forward with His arm inside of my arm while we talked.

He said, "To strengthen you, I'm holding your arms up. When you get tired or discouraged, know that I'm behind you covering your back side from being hit by arrows. I'm in you, filling you with Me. I draw love from My Father."

I felt such a powerful drawing of love from God going into Jesus who was standing in my spot, in my body. He had no problem drawing love from the Father. Jesus has no barriers or walls or fear but is like an open channel.

Jesus said, "I look to the Father, and what I see Him doing in the spirit, I do! Don't look with your natural eyes. I don't see what you see. I see spirit realms. When you minister or do anything, then say, "Jesus, step into me." And then let your hand do what My hand wants to do. Let your mouth move and let My words and thoughts come out.

"At times I'll wait to see what My Father is doing, and then I'll do that. Let your vessel do what I'm supposed to do. I'll draw love from the Father, through your hand vessel and it will flow into them, if you'll do it! I'll draw power from God, and take it through your vessel, and it will go and do the will of the Father. No problem!"

Then Jesus stepped out of me, and we continued walking, holding hands on the beach.

Jesus wants us to know that we don't have to be afraid. He wants unity with us like it states in Isaiah 41:10:

> Fear not [there is nothing to fear], for I am with you; do not look around you in terror and be dismayed, for I am your God. I will strengthen and harden you to difficulties, yes, I will help you; yes, I will hold you up and retain you with My [victorious] right hand of rightness and justice.

Jesus wants us to know that we are one with Him like what John 14:20 says:

> At that time [when that day comes] you will know [for yourselves] that I am in My Father, and you [are] in Me, and I [am] in you.

In Colossians 1:26-27 it talks about the mystery of Christ in us:

> The mystery of which was hidden for ages and generations [from angels and men], but is now revealed to His holy people (the saints), To whom God was pleased to make known how great for the Gentiles are the riches of the glory of this mystery, which is Christ within and among you, the Hope of [realizing the] glory.

2001-2010

The Money Room

My ex-husband and I owned a photography business at that time, and we got into some financial problems. We had just received a call that said, "We have put a freeze on your bank account; you have twenty-four hours to come up with $30,000 or we will come and put a padlock on your doors and begin the process of getting our payments." We didn't have $30.00, let alone $30,000 and we had no one we could go to who could loan us the money. Just imagine the shock of knowing that the only money we had was the $2.50 in our pocket right then!

Knowing there was nothing else I could do, I went home and began to worship Jesus—not realizing what was about to happen! I was in the middle of worshiping Jesus when He said, "Sit still. I have something to show and tell you." I sat down on the floor and got comfortable. Then I heard Him say, "Come up here. I have something to show you." And I felt part of my spirit ascending.

I saw Jesus standing beside me (I was an adult) and He gave me a big hug and kissed me on the cheek. Holding hands, we began walking toward a huge door. I noticed a large wheel-type door handle, like what you would see on an old bank vault. I had never seen one except in old movies.

The door was open, so we went in. Jesus stood to the side to let me go in first—He is always a gentleman! When I entered, I saw rows and rows as far as you could see. I looked to the left and still rows and rows. I looked to the right and still more and more rows. I began to be curious and started to focus in on these rows. Then I could see it—these were rows and rows of money, piles and stacks of money! I realized this was a good place to be right now!

Jesus asked me, "Do you want to see your pile?" I quickly said, "Yes!"

We walked over to separate piles of neatly stacked money. I saw my name, my two girls' names, and my husband's name, all on individual piles. Each person's pile was about three cubic feet—full of stacks of cash *money*! My stacks were about three feet high, some stacks were two and a half feet high, some two feet high, some half a foot high, but still all the piles were about three feet square.

He asked me, "How much do you need?"

With all the faith I could pull up from the bottom of my being, I breathlessly mustered out with a lot of embarrassment, "$30,000," knowing that it was probably all the money in my pile.

Jesus said, "OK," and leaned over. He took a pinch of money about a half-inch thick and put it in my hand. Now I was really embarrassed, realizing that all the faith I could muster up was only a pinch to Jesus as He handed me $30,000+!

I folded my fingers over my seemingly small, yet huge to me, handful of money, trying to figure out how to get this back! You know, where do you put it? I didn't have a pocket and I wasn't carrying a purse with me.

Jesus said, "Do you want to know how to get it back?"

I said, "Yes." And instantly there was an angel standing against the left wall. Jesus pointed to Him and said, "Go!" He took off like a shot, jetting out the vault door. I didn't know where He was going or how, but I sure was hoping it had something to do with the money!

I looked back at the stacks and asked, because I noticed some of them were short, "Do they ever run out?" Jesus laughed – not at me, but only because to Him that was a funny question.

He said, "No, it never runs out." Then He leaned down and put His hand under the shortest stack and the other hand on top and slid the shorter stack to the side. It instantly filled back up with money, level with the others.

Jesus asked, "Do you know how to get the money here in these piles?"

I said, "No."

He said, *"By tithing, giving offerings, by finding (or quoting) scriptures that pertain to finances, by faith ... and just because I love."*

I thought, "There are people who have never been taught about tithing or giving or faith, so how do they get money when they need it?"

He said, "By My grace and mercy and just because I love them!"

I noticed my daughter's pile. At that time she was only about one and a half years old, and her stacks were mostly even but some stacks were shorter. I asked, "Why are some of her stacks shorter? She knows nothing and has never tithed or given an offering and certainly hasn't quoted any scriptures."

Jesus said, "But she still has needs. She still needed a baby crib, diapers, food, and clothes. She also has money here for her ministry when she needs it!"

The funny part of this is what I noticed out of the corner of my eye: I saw a big pile of money to the right side of us and read a certain pastor's name on it. I had just heard that this certain pastor had not been handling the church finances correctly, and I was very upset with him at that time.

While I was looking at his pile I realized it was bigger than mine, and that really upset me! I don't know if I had my hands on my hips, my mouth open, or my lower lip stuck out or what, but Jesus grinned and said, "His needs are bigger than yours." Jesus never commented on my attitude. We then walked out of the vault.

The next day a lady called us and said she had heard that we wanted to sell a portion of the store. She had $35,000 cash and could have it put in our bank account by noon, if we were interested.

We said, "Yes!" (Notice we had more than enough!)

We were able to buy her out a year later and got our store back.

His riches are far above anything I could have thought or imagined, just like it says in Philippians 4:19, "And my God will liberally supply your every need according to His riches in glory in Christ Jesus."

Jesus Is My Shepherd

After praying in the spirit (in tongues, Acts 2:4) for a while, I began to quiet myself and felt a drawing to Jesus. I stepped over, as an adult, to meet Him face to face. We hugged and He smiled and was so happy to see me. We began to walk along a river with thick, deep, rich tall grass that blew gently in the breeze.

Jesus said, "The grass ahead is green and lush. It's full of life and virtue." I could see it was long and green, thick, and full of life. The river that flowed from the spring was clean, fresh, and sweet. I bent down to taste the water – scooping some up in my hands I noticed it was sweet and sparkling and so full of life.

The air was peaceful and full of music, even without instruments. I could hear birds singing. I saw a large slanted rock and as we came up to it, I just climbed up. I was wearing pants, not a robe or dress, so I sat down and dangled my feet off the edge. I felt the soft green grass blow across my bare feet.

"We will meet here," Jesus said.

Jesus sat up next to me said, "I am your Shepherd. You don't have to fear the future. Trust Me! Trust Me. You don't have to fear the future. What kind of Shepherd would I be if I didn't lead you to where there was provision? I wouldn't lead you to where you'd fall into danger and be hurt. But I will protect you and guide you. You don't have to fear the future—trust My leading! For the future is good, sweet, and full of life. Trust Me! I am your Shepherd. Come back to the rock and meet Me here."

Never forget Jesus will guide us just like it says in Revelation 7:17:

> "For the Lamb Who is in the midst of the throne will be their Shepherd, and He will guide them to the springs of the waters of life; and God will wipe away every tear from their eyes."

Let's Fly with Jesus

A photography studio we had built next to our house became my new prayer room. This night, after a long day of doing a family shoot, I just enjoyed the seclusion of our three acres and the peace and quiet of the building. Turning on the air conditioner and some soaking music, I sat down on the soft, carpeted floor and began focusing on the love of Jesus and the Father. I felt the Holy Spirit drawing me to the spirit realm ... instantly, Jesus was standing there, eager to spend time with me.

After we hugged, Jesus said, "You need to have some fun!" This time I appeared as a teenager. He took me by the hand, and we walked through a soft, grassy field filled with flowers and then we stopped at the edge of a cliff. He turned to me and smiled, and I just knew we were going to get to fly again.

We both turned and jumped off the cliff and flew. I realized by just knowing, that this was a new "Flying Game." Jesus and I flew without wings, dodging in and out of obstacles, chasing each other over hills and trees, and dive bombing into water and back up again.

He said, "I have many things planned for the ones who love Me—for those who stay until the end!"

> He has made everything beautiful and appropriate in its time. He has also planted eternity [a sense of divine purpose] in the human heart [a mysterious longing which nothing under the sun can satisfy, except God]— yet man cannot find out (comprehend, grasp) what God has done (His overall plan) from the beginning to the end. (Ecclesiastes 3:11)

Heaven Is Real, and I'm Coming Back

This morning I woke up with the song "I Love You Lord and I Lift My Voice" going through my mind. I sang it, and the presence of God fell on me.

I began to cry, and He said, "You're to tell them I'm coming back, Heaven is real, and they are not ready. I'm coming back and they are not ready!"

> "But while they were going away to buy, the bridegroom came, and those who were prepared went in with him to the marriage feast; and the door was shut." (Matthew 25:1)

Light Heals

Lying on the floor in the portrait studio, which was now my new prayer room, I was spending time worshiping when I saw Jesus wrapped in light. It was like this light had a substance and was wrapped around Him. I wasn't afraid to walk right into Him so I ran and jumped into His arms.

Jesus said, "The light heals—open up and let the light heal you." This reminded me of Daniel 2:22 that says, "He reveals the deep and secret things. He knows what is in the darkness, and the light dwells with Him."

As He hugged me I felt as though a waterfall was flowing over me. I felt so refreshed and made whole. All bitterness, worry, disappointment, and discouragement that I didn't even know I was carrying until I came into the light of Jesus, was gone. It's clear that this time I was an adult in Heaven.

Notice in Malachi the freedom came after the healing:

> But for you who revere my name, the sun of righteousness will rise with healing in its rays (wings). And you will go out and frolic like well-fed calves. (Malachi 4:2 NIV)

Jesus' appearance on this visit reminded me of what happens during a solar eclipse; it looks as if the moon is dark and wrapped with light. Jesus was a bright light, but there was a brighter light wrapped around Him.

Eyes to See

After spending the day raking fall leaves and cleaning up the supper dishes, I went out to the studio/prayer room to pray and to spend time with Jesus. I felt such peace! Joy and love came into the room and covered me. Instantly I was in the spirit realm as an adult. Jesus met me and we hugged. I noticed we were standing on sand, and as we turned around to walk, I saw an ocean. Jesus and I held hands like lovers would, and we walked on the beach by this ocean in Heaven, laughing and talking.

He was saying, "Yes, you've been given access into My Father's presence."

I asked about the beings in the throne room, "Why do all the beings around God's throne have eyes all over them?"

Jesus said, "To see the praises and to see what's coming. The atmosphere around the Father is like an eye shape, radiating the power of God. The reason Satan attacks eyes is because the eyes remind Him of what is in Heaven, and He can't see any more. He no longer has eyes to see with."

Jesus said, "Pray for eyes. It will become common for you: for the blind to receive their sight."

Then I saw a gigantic rock rising up from the sand, and I stood on top of it, at the edge of this huge rock. Jesus was on my right and asked, "Do you trust Me?"

I said, "Yes." He took my hand, and we walked off the edge into the air and kept walking.

Jesus said, "You walked on what you cannot see. Hold My hand and you will walk on substance that you cannot see! When you pray for the crippled and the blind, take My hand and walk on toward them. Your Heaven will be filled with pictures of when you trusted Me!"

He continued, "Your house in Heaven will be filled with memories of when you were so afraid but still trusted in Me and how I came through, and manifested the glory of our Father. When you walk in uncertainty and can't see where to go, and you hear the evil on all sides, keep a hold of My hand. Put your head down and trust that I will lead you through because I *can* see!"

When you are frustrated, don't forget what John says:

> The godless world can't take him in because it doesn't have eyes to see him, doesn't know what to look for. But you know him already because He has been staying with you, and will even be in you! (John 14:15 MSG)

Rose Petals Falling

While I was praying, the Holy Spirit took me into the spirit realm and I appeared as a teen and saw rose petals falling all over me. It was like someone was showering me with thick, soft, fragrant rose petals. I could sense Jesus was enjoying watching me dance and twirl around in the falling petals.

I saw a covering over me like a canopy, but the petals were falling down from under the canopy. They were so thick and fragrant, and there were so many, and I felt very loved and beautiful.

2011

Fragrance of Jesus

During a worship service in church, I could see the fragrance of Jesus coming up from us as a body of worshipers. It was going up rapidly, fast and strong, wide and thick, like light and with energy waves. It was going up into God's throne room. God leaned back and breathed in the fragrance of His Son Jesus, and He was very pleased.

Jesus said, "It's not that important where this church moves because My fragrance will go with you."

We are a sweet fragrance to the Father like it says in 2 Corinthians 2:15–16:

> For we are the sweet fragrance of Christ [which exhales] unto God, [discernible alike] among those who are being saved … it is an aroma from life to life [a vital fragrance, living and fresh].

Thick Gel

While worshiping, I was taken to Heaven and introduced to some people about whom Jesus said, "These are your friends. When you feel rejected, come here and play. Here you are accepted." Then I felt a thick, wonderful gel-like substance cover me.

Jesus said, "This gel soaks in and fills the hurts and cracks of life, like it would to an old wineskin — it softens the hurts and wounds. Come here and get healed and play with your friends."

The people began patting me and hugging me and saying, "We are so happy you're one of us!" This thick gel reminded me of a passage in Jeremiah 46:11 that says, "Go up to Gilead and obtain [healing] balm, O Virgin Daughter of Egypt!"

Snow Sledding with Jesus

I turned on some soft worship music, sat down, quieted my mind, and soaked in the presence of Jesus. I stepped over into the spirit realm by faith. I was in Heaven as an adult this time. Jesus met me, and we began to walk in the crystal-clean, white snow. As soon as we began to walk, I noticed the snow was thick flakes and was so soft and fluffy. I wasn't cold. We kicked the snow up in the air and watched it float down; it made music. Each little flake made music.

Then Jesus bent down, gathered up some snow and made a ball—He threw it at me and ran! I was really surprised! I didn't know He liked to play and have fun! So I made a snowball and began to chase Jesus around a tree and other obstacles until I hit Him right in the middle of the back. He acted like He was shot and fell face first with arms out, falling into the snow. As I ran by Him, He grabbed me and we rolled around playing. Then we got up and ran through the snow. The snow in Heaven didn't clump up and get hard, but you could still make a ball and have snowball fights. The snow is cool but not cold.

Next, we were immediately at the top of a snowy mountain. In no time, I was holding a rope to a red sled and Jesus had a blue sled.

He asked, "Do you want to go sledding?"

I said, "Oh yeah!" I was a little scared because it was so steep and long, like a ski mountain.

Jesus said, "I'll go first, OK?"

I asked, "How do I steer this?"

He laughed and said, "With your feet like the old ones." He jumped on His sled and took off. I could hear Him laughing as he rode down with fluffy snow flying up in His face.

I jumped on my sled and over the edge I went. It wasn't cold at all, and I was having a great time! I plowed through snowdrifts and they would come up and hit me in the face liked a puff. We were on something like a skateboard track but with snow. We went up one side, back down, and then up to the other side. We stopped, laughed, and hugged.

Jesus said, "You don't have to walk back up the mountain to go again," and we were instantly at the top of the mountain.

Jesus asked, "Do you want to go again?"

I said, "I'll go first!" So I got on and down I went. I leaned left and it became like a toboggan track up one side, then across, and sliding up the other side. Jesus was on a trail that crossed above me to the right and then over me and down. I took the next track, and we crisscrossed over each other until we made it to the bottom. It was so much fun! When I got off, we hugged and laughed and twirled and laughed some more. It was exhilarating!

Suddenly the snow was gone and there was tall, thick, soft green grass. We walked and talked for a while, holding hands. Jesus loves to slowly walk and talk. We walked by a beach and a lake and then sat on a mountain ledge overlooking the lake.

Jesus said, "I know this is your favorite place." Then He reached into me and pulled out some flowers from the inside of my heart. I was sitting there, kind of shocked at what just happened but I felt as if I was transparent when He did that; it didn't hurt at all. He said, "Your heart smells of Me, but I'm going to put in more of Me." He smiled and put more beautiful flowers in my heart! The most important thing you can do is learn to love like Jesus.

Playing with Jesus

And walk in love, [esteeming and delighting in one another] as Christ loved us and gave Himself up for us, a slain offering and sacrifice to God [for you, so that it became] a sweet fragrance. (Ephesians 5:2)

Tree House/Slide with Jesus

One night while I was worshiping, Jesus said, "Come here. You need to have fun." I appeared as an adult and Jesus began to walk across a plank that was forty-plus feet up from the ground! I followed Him and we went into a hole and began to climb.

I said, "We are in a tree house!"

Jesus said, "It's a tree slide!"

Jesus went into the slide hands first. I went in hands first too, but later, I turned to put my feet first. We slid down on our stomachs through these loopy-loops. We slid over water and through soft snow drifts that would 'poof' as we went through them. We slid through piles of multi-colored fall leaves, over the ocean, and then even rode the waves on this slide!

"Talk about virtual reality!" Jesus said, laughing.

We slid way down over hills and ski slopes, banked corners, went through balls, like you'd find in a kid's ball pit, and finally slid to a stop.

Jesus was standing there laughing hard and He hugged me.

He said, "Did you like that? Man, that was fun! And there were no lines to stand in!"

Lying with Jesus

Going into my prayer room again (my portrait studio), I turned on the heater. I turned on some soft worship music, fervently wanting to see Jesus to spend time talking and walking with Him. I began to worship.

The Holy Spirit soon took me to Jesus. Jesus and I (as a teen) walked and then lay together under some tall green trees with soft, tall, flowing, green grass. I was on my back with my head on His stomach. He ran His fingers through my hair.

Jesus said, "The tree doesn't struggle to be a tree because that's what it is designed to do. The grass doesn't struggle to be grass because that's what it's designed to do. Do what comes natural for you because that's what you're designed to do. If you're struggling, then do something different. Do what you're designed to do." The word of God instructs us to stop struggling.

> Stop toiling and doing and producing for the food that perishes and decomposes … the Son of Man will give (furnish) you that, for God the Father has authorized and certified Him and put His seal of endorsement upon Him. (John 6:27)

Floating in the River

While worshiping, I went to Heaven and a tall black-haired guy stood to my right with a gentle stream running in front of us.

He said, "Come on, Sis, get in!" I asked Jesus who He was, and Jesus said, "That's your brother." (I had always wanted a brother.)

Brother was walking in the water, laughing. I was a teen with bare feet and just stepped in. The water was cool (not cold) and refreshing as it ran over my feet. The water felt like it was energized with life and it made my feet tingle. The tingling ran up my legs and body.

Brother was ahead saying, "Come on!"

As I walked on some smooth, round rocks I began to crave more water to run over me. The water began to get deeper, and it energized me, tingled, and felt so good. I began to splash it over me and then I knelt down. I couldn't get deep enough! I lay on my stomach in the river as it washed over me with this tingling, energizing, life-giving feeling. I put my head under the water and wanted it to cover my ears, eyes, and heart.

Then I saw Brother floating in the stream, so I turned over on my back. The river had so much life in it, it carried me. I floated under flowers that were hanging over the shore; they formed a tunnel.

Jesus laughed and said, "It's like your log flume rides on earth!" I knew He meant the ones in Silver Dollar City in Branson, Missouri.

He said, "The river comes and goes from the throne of God." I looked downstream, and other people were floating, enjoying the life-giving river. I could hear other people, they were standing on a bridge ahead of me, watching us and laughing.

A little boy waved to me as I floated by and said, "Hi, Kim!"

An older man said to the boy, "Shhhh, she's resting in the river," and the little boy quietly waved to me and gave me a sweet smile. I could hear kids laughing and playing, babies giggling, and cats purring.

I looked up and saw the throne of God to my right. He (God) was watching me, smiling and laughing at my enjoyment. I floated under His throne and back out. I floated under some huge weeping willow trees that were growing beside the river. I saw some men leaning over an architectural table, planning how to build a mansion for someone who was coming.

One said, "Kim likes chairs like this and trees like this (waving to me). We know she likes weeping willows, so she has nice big ones at her place."

I then saw Peal (my horse) standing on the shore. She nuzzled me as I was floating by and said, "We don't ride today. Today you are to rest in the river." Water in Heaven is like a thick Jell-O and baby oil mixture, it's thick and slippery, and it's filled with so much life it tingles on the skin.

Then I found myself once again in my prayer room. I quickly went inside the house to take a bath, to make a comparison. I then realized how flat, lifeless, dull, and non-energizing the water really is on our earth.

Later, while lying in bed, I felt myself stepping over in the spirit and straightaway I was standing under a waterfall with the same kind of water as the river. It flowed over me from head to toe. It was thick and it tingled but it was a natural-flowing waterfall. I'm guessing all the water in Heaven is like this – thick, tingly, life-giving water. This event makes the word of God come alive for me.

> He leads me beside quiet waters, He restores my soul. (Psalm 23:2)

> …water flowing from the temple ankle deep, knee deep, waist deep.(Ezekiel 47:1–12)

Body Surfing

While my body was asleep, I felt my spirit step out, and Jesus and I were suddenly body surfing on high, wonderful, fun waves in Heaven. I was a teenager in this experience.

Jump; Just Jump

During worship in my prayer room, I was instantly in Heaven, and I was watching a guy. He walked to the edge of a huge waterfall. As I watched him, he didn't even hesitate or look for a half second before he jumped over the edge and began to fall. Somehow I knew he had never seen this waterfall. He had no idea what possible danger was under the water, and yet he didn't hesitate before jumping. And all of a sudden 'he' turned into *me*! *I* was floating in this extremely fast current and it was so much fun! I gently floated up to the shore unharmed.

Jesus said, "Jump—just jump out there. It will be fun; just jump! Don't analyze it—just jump!"

Jump, Jump

Instantly, Jesus and I were sitting on a ledge behind this huge waterfall. The water was falling down fifteen to twenty feet in front of us as we sat behind it. There was a swimming hole-like pool that extended from the rocks all the way down to where the waterfall touched the river, and we were watching kids play in this pool beneath us.

Jesus said, "I have stuff to do, but I make time to sit and watch my kids play." Then He said, "Jump, jump!" So I jumped off and went way, way down about 200 feet and plunged under the water, laughing. Like all the sports I'd done in Heaven, it was so much fun!

Jesus said, "Time is speeding up. Jump; just jump!"

I knew Jesus was talking about instant obedience, and I felt drawn to the deep roaring of the waterfall.

[Roaring] deep calls to [roaring] deep at the thunder of Your waterspouts; all Your breakers and Your rolling waves have gone over me. (Psalm 42:7)

Behold, to obey is better than sacrifice, and to hearken than the fat of rams. (1 Samuel 15:22)

Don't Be Afraid of the Future

During worship, Jesus took me to a white garden where the flowers made an arch. I, as an adult, and Jesus walked through it. Then as I looked up I could see buildings that were covered in white flowers.

As we lay down and were looking up, Jesus leaned over to me and looked in my eyes and said, "You're afraid of a lot of things, but don't be afraid. I will take care of you! I will take care of you. Trust Me!"

Then we flew through something like a red tunnel, and I saw houses in the future. They had a canopy-like enclosure that covered the houses and yards. The way we have automatic gates, these transparent canopies had doors to let the cars go in. People were watering the grass inside theses canopies. Sidewalks were even enclosed. It was very space-age looking! Odd for sure; like the show, "The Jetsons."

Jesus Is Fun

While I was worshiping, Jesus said, "Open your eyes." In the spirit I opened my eyes (I was an adult) and could see Jesus clearly. He was a different color than before—and instantly He was on a horse and said, "Come on."

Peal, my horse, was right there and I jumped on and began to pet his super soft hair. I cried because he was so soft. Things in Heaven are so overwhelming.

Jesus and I rode through a field of brightly colored flowers. Then we dismounted and walked as flowers (so fragrant with thick, soft petals) began to fall heavily around us. At that point I walked right into the thickest honeysuckle patch you've ever seen. The plants were taller than I am and so thick that I couldn't see through them.

I asked Jesus, "Why all the flowers? Shouldn't I be interceding or casting down demonic forces or something?"

Jesus said, "I'm doing this for you because you like flowers, and this is fun. I like to have fun. That's why men are into fun – it is part of My character. The other stuff is easily done, such as healing and casting down demonic strongholds. They (men) don't worry; they like to have fun."

Jesus said, "No prayer ever goes empty. The hours, days, months, and years you've prayed are not in vain."

And *then* we walked into the future. I remember seeing lots of people looking and listening to me. You see, I had been struggling with how long it was taking: that is, me getting to tell people about Heaven. But I think Jesus' main point of taking me into the future was to show that it's easy to travel in Heaven.

Jesus said, "No matter what you do on earth, nothing will be as fast or as quick as it is here since time is not a challenge here. Follow your heart and don't wait for an anointing or a voice. Follow your heart. That's why your heart must stay healed from bitterness and stay tender. Faith comes by love so follow your heart and if you see a need in people, then pray for them!"

Soon afterward we sat on something that looked and felt like a gel-filled cloud, and we used it as a chair! Jesus said, "It's soft and conforming" (like it was gel mixed with air.) He said, "I think something similar could be made on earth: gel-puffed chairs with blown air that you could hang in the house."

Expensive Perfume

I was sitting on the floor worshiping and soaking when all of a sudden I saw Jesus. He was giving very expensive bottles of perfume to only a few people.

I appeared in Heaven as an adult and was thinking, "Wow, that's extremely expensive stuff and it's a huge bottle." He sat one on my chair and I thought, "Oh, no. He's put it on the wrong chair!" I tried to move it to someone else's chair or give it to someone beside me, thinking He couldn't, in any way, have meant it for me.

He put it back on my chair and I tried to explain to Him, "You've made a mistake; that's my chair!"

He said, "I know. It's for you!" and smiled. I was stunned that Jesus would give me such an expensive perfume and such a huge bottle.

Jesus said, "I'm covering you with a good smell so that you'll smell good to others."

Then during worship at church one morning I saw the bottle floating in front of me, and Jesus squirted me. I felt such peace and confidence. He said, "You smell good!"

Notice that at the time Jesus gave himself up for us, in Ephesians, it says He was a fragrant offering. When we do things for others, does that smell good to our Father? Yes, I think it does!

> "Christ loved us and gave himself up for us as a fragrant offering and sacrifice to GOD." (Ephesians 5:2)

Whirlwind

During the worship service at church, I stopped singing to Jesus and began receiving from Him. I felt a whirlwind around me and it reminded me of 2 Kings 2:11:

> As they still went on and talked, behold, a chariot of fire and horses of fire parted the two of them, and Elijah went up by a whirlwind into Heaven.

Still during worship, I saw a deep royal blue horizon coming closer. Then I saw Jesus standing in the whirlwind (in my church), dressed in a royal blue robe. He stood there smiling, enjoying the people's praise as it was rising up to the Father.

Water Volcano

Jesus took me to a high mountain.

He said, "I don't bring many here." Jesus and I were above the top of the mountain, at the tip. Looking down into it we saw water spew up forcefully and then run gently down the sides of the mountain, like a volcano.

I asked, "How does the water come up this high to spew out with such power like that?"

Jesus said, "When you get in my 'flow,' then the river that is inside of you is full and ready to overflow and it will just come up and out."

It was a beautiful mountaintop. I could see the water flowing down with sprays of water to bring life to the lush green ravine. A misty dew was rolling up on both sides, it was gorgeous and very peaceful. The way the river flowed up reminded me of John 4:14:

> But whoever takes a drink of the water that I will give him shall never, no never, be thirsty any more. But the water

that I will give him shall become a spring of water welling up (flowing, bubbling) [continually] within him unto (into, for) eternal life.

Jesus Does the Cha-Cha

I saw Jesus dancing with people in Heaven doing a dance similar to the Cha-Cha. He said to me (I was an adult), "Come and join us. There's no heaviness here, the weight of the world isn't on us! Relax and do what comes naturally for you!"

Flower Petals

During worship I was caught up, and I was placed in a gondola, like those in Venice with Jesus riding in the back looking at me (I was a teenager). He said, "I want to serenade you." However, I was so full of worship and admiration for Jesus that I stood up in the boat and sang from my heart to Him.

He said, "I have a gift for you!" I saw a large blue bow hanging in the air. I reached up and untied it. Thick fragrant flower petals came pouring out all over me!

Dancing around His Throne

Another time during worship, I saw Jesus sitting on a throne. I (as an adult) danced around His throne with others who were there. We were holding a long ribbon, dancing and worshiping Jesus.

Precious Jewels

Jesus and I sat on a bed. He hugged me and said, "Don't worry about tomorrow. It will be good." I felt Him pouring gold and pearls into me.

Jesus said, "I am pouring in great and precious jewels because pearls of a great price have been paid. You tell of Heaven, and those who don't believe won't step over into the spirit realm to see. But when they finally come home they will be surprised when they do finally see!"

> And the servant brought forth jewels of silver, and jewels of gold, and raiment, and gave them to Rebekah. He gave also to her brother and to her mother precious things. (Genesis 24:53)

2012

Walk through Pictures

During worship, I walked into an art gallery in Heaven as an adult. (I had never been to an art gallery at this point in life.) I saw a large framed picture of flowers but they were *real* and moving with a breeze in the picture. I leaned forward and smelled the flowers in the picture. I wanted to put the picture in my mansion. I took it down and instantly I was at my mansion where I hung it on the wall, still noticing that the flowers kept moving.

And then instantly I was back at the art gallery. Jesus showed me a picture of a waterfall. I wanted that one too, so instantly we were back at my mansion where Jesus hung it on my wall. I noticed the waterfall was real and the water was really falling, but it didn't fill up the picture with water.

I heard Daddy say, "Watch this and go into it!" I walked into the picture and was at the waterfall. I also walked into the picture of flowers and immediately walked among those flowers. I walked into a picture of a beach and right away, I was on that beach with Jesus.

Jesus said, "If you want to come back here, then you, and others, can come here!" Suddenly a lady was standing beside me, and we were looking at a rollercoaster picture. We looked at each other and walked through it and got on the rollercoaster ride. We rode it together, got off, and laughed about how fun it was. Father God has great things planned for us like it says in 1 Corinthians 2:9.

> But, on the contrary, as the Scripture says, What eye has not seen and ear has not heard and has not entered into the heart of man, [all that] God has prepared (made and keeps ready) for those who love Him [who hold Him in affectionate reverence, promptly obeying Him and gratefully recognizing the benefits He has bestowed].

Jesus in a Bar

Sitting on my red leather rocking recliner, looking out the front window and watching the deer drink out of our bird bath, I felt drawn to spend time with Jesus. Going out to my studio, which was now my prayer room, I turned on some worship music and sat down on the floor. After about thirty to forty-five minutes of worshiping, I saw Jesus as a bright light and I felt myself walk into His light!

He said, "Walk with Me." As He held my right hand we walked down a hall toward a bright white light and into a bar (I was an adult). Jesus walked on one side of the bar and I walked on the other side, and we were watching the people.

He said, "You see them as sinning. I see them as My righteousness that hasn't come yet. When it comes, what's wrong is made "right." The wounded heart becomes healed and demons flee. They drink because of wounds, thoughts, and past hurts but when My righteousness covers them, the wounds become healed and made right, and they stop sinning."

Jesus said, "The man at the pool was bitter and kept rehearsing and telling of His wounded heart, which affected His body. When I healed His heart, it affected His body" (John 5:1–6). Jesus, not condemning, reminded me of John 8:4, 11–12.

> They said, "This woman has been caught in the very act of adultery." (Did Jesus condemn her? No!) ... and Jesus said, "I do not condemn you either. Go on your way and from now on sin no more." Once more Jesus addressed the crowd. He said, "I am the Light of the world. He who follows Me will not be walking in the dark, but will have the Light which is Life."

The High Praise Room with Blue Crystals

Jesus took me to a blue crystal room in Heaven called the High Praise Room. He enthusiastically said, "The people who are uninhibited in singing praise to Him create this room. Their uninhibited praise from the gut, with everything in them, that is not for show, has created the room."

He continued, "These High Praise rooms could be created when someone is riding a horse, a motorcycle, a hang glider, or when from different countries, they're speaking in different languages during a service, and so forth. It is extreme praise that forms this blue crystal room."

I noticed as I stood in the room that each crystal replays the person's enthusiastic praise. Your enthusiastic praise will be played continuously forever!

He said, "It doesn't have to be on key or a long song; it's from the uninhibited spontaneous heart!"

"And David danced before the Lord with all His might, clad in a linen ephod [a priest's upper garment]." (2 Samuel 6:14)

Doing Nothing with Jesus

During worship, Jesus came to me, took my hand, and said, "Let's go walk by the spring." In Heaven the flowers grow thick along the river, the trees are also very full there. The water is also thick, full, and shiny. We began to skip rocks. I was an adult.

Jesus said, "The round, smooth ones skip better because there is no resistance," as He threw a rock and it plopped. He laughed, then picked up another one, and waited for me to go. I threw mine and it skipped big hops across the water and He said, "Good one!"

We sat down in the grass after skipping rocks for some time, laughing and enjoying being together. I picked a flower to smell and Jesus said, "Listen to it!" I did, and it made music out of its pores. Even the grass made music!

I asked, "How could it make music?"

Jesus said, "Because it has life, and everything that has life produces. If a heart doesn't have life, it doesn't produce. If a dream doesn't have life, it doesn't produce. If a relationship doesn't have life, it doesn't produce. When you pray for people, call forth life."

We lay back in the grass and Jesus said, "I enjoy doing nothing with you. Just being with you makes me happy. Just like today when you were with your daughter and grandkids, you didn't really do anything; it was just fun doing nothing together."

While I was sitting with Jesus, my nose kept itching in the natural. I'd have to go from being in the spirit realm with Jesus, to the natural realm to scratch my nose, and then back to being with Jesus again. I had to do it about six or seven times.

Jesus said, "You can operate in the spirit realm and the natural realm at the same time, they are that close to each other."

Then Daddy God took me back to the blue crystal room. Every piece of blue crystal hanging down from the ceiling and off the walls sang with incredible life and energy. He had told me that whatever you do, do it with all you've got. These blue crystals are created each time someone on earth worships Him with everything they've got. They are a memorial for someone on earth who gives their talent totally uninhibited for Him. Nothing someone does goes unnoticed by Him. He knows everything about us just like it says in Psalm 138:4–6 (MSG):

> When they hear what you have to say, God, all earth's kings will say "Thank you." They'll sing of what you've done: "How great the glory of God!" And here's why: God, high above, sees far below; no matter the distance, he knows everything about us.

Cloud of Witnesses Say, "Go-Go-Go"

This morning I turned on praise and worship music and almost instantly I was in Heaven. I found myself standing on a stage as an adult, with Jesus to my left. There was a crowd of people in front, cheering for me. I was at a point in my life with many decisions to make.

They began to shout, "Go-Go-Go-Go-Go-Go!"

Jesus said, "Here there are a lot of graduations!"

Please examine the following passage, and remember that we are always surrounded by witnesses.

> Therefore then, since we are surrounded by so great a cloud of witnesses [who have borne testimony to the Truth], let us strip off and throw aside every encumbrance (unnecessary weight) and that sin which so readily (deftly and cleverly) clings to and entangles us, and let us run

with patient endurance and steady and active persistence the appointed course of the race that is set before us. (Hebrews 12:12)

Gondola Boat Ride with Jesus

I was praying when suddenly Jesus and I were in a gondola boat again. I was a teen, and He put large white gardenias around my neck and began to sing to me. He sang about how I was His number 1, and His first choice. I felt incredibly loved, wanted, and accepted, looking into His beautiful eyes and feeling His tender touch. Jesus paddled and steered the gondola boat and said, "Relax and enjoy the ride. Remember I am the one paddling and I am the one steering so you don't have to push your way though. I have great plans for you and this is only the beginning. Therefore you can lie back and enjoy the ride. I am in control!" He laughed and kept slowly paddling.

Daddy and Mama Are Solid/Park and Swings

I saw a gold and red ring around the ceiling, and I went up into it. It circled me, then wrapped around me like a candy cane. I was a child. I saw

Daddy God and He said, "It covers you with sweetness. You are one of my 'Candy Stripers,'" and He laughed.

Later I was playing with Jesus at a park. Jesus was pushing me on the swings. I looked up to see where the soft rope-like things were attached, but they seemed like they just kept going up into the sky and were not attached to anything.

We stood and played in a field of flowers, laughing and talking. Then Jesus and I played in the spring, splashing in the water. After that, I just stood motionless in the water.

Jesus said, "The family is strong. Daddy is happy; the family is solid. Daddy and Mama love each other; there is lots of love and they laugh together and play. You can go run, it's OK. You can go run and not have to feel like you have to provide for yourself. Life is solid at home; you can go run and do what you're supposed to do freely and with confidence that there's love, and the family at home is solid. Go and run freely with confidence." I felt heat blow on me, and then the need to provide for myself left. (I knew He meant Daddy and Mama were God and Holy Spirit.)

At the same time, He was healing me from the past hurts I had from my parents, even though I did not know I needed to be healed. I felt freedom and a release from fear, and then Jesus and I played in the river again. This event reminded me of a happy family in Acts 16:34 (EXB):

> After this the jailer took Paul and Silas home and gave them food. He and his family [household] were very happy [rejoiced; celebrated] because they now believed in God.

Jesus' Courtyard

During worship I saw little blue angels flying around me, like little round blue dots. Then right away, Jesus and I (as a teenager) were in a courtyard where people were set up in a circle, painting and drawing on easels. There were fresh fruit and vegetable stands, crafts, flowers, and a huge fresh market in this courtyard.

Jesus said, "This is My courtyard."

I said, "I have never seen anything like this!"

Jesus replied while laughing, "You didn't ask! If you like to paint, draw, and do crafts, you will still get to do that in Heaven. If you like fresh flowers and fruit markets, they will be in Heaven for you to enjoy." Let it be on earth as it is in Heaven.

> And when these days were expired, the king made a feast unto all the people that were present in Shushan the palace, both unto great and small, seven days, in the court of the garden of the king's palace; There were white, green, and blue, hangings, fastened with cords of fine linen, and purple to silver rings, and pillars of marble. The beds were of gold and silver, upon a pavement of red, blue, white, and black marble. (Esther 1:5-6 KJV)

Wrapped in His Presence

Jesus took me to a throne in Heaven. I was with Jesus as an adult, and I was *in* Jesus. When Jesus sat next to the Father, I sat next to the Father because I was in Jesus, and He was in me. We watched as children and others danced in worship before them. I noticed no one sat down in chairs or pews like we do in a church service.

Then I noticed something like a clear bubble that wrapped around me, like plastic food storage wrap would wrap around some food. Daddy said, "When you reach out, it is like a clear see-through wrap that covers your hands and arms." As I reached out to the people, the Father was the one touching them. As I reached out, I was touching others with the Father's presence wrapped around me. Now, I cover myself with His presence; I am wrapped in His presence. We who are in Christ, are hidden in His presence.

Jesus said, "I and the Father are one." (John 10:30)

> Even if you do not believe me, believe the miracles that you know and understand that the Father is in Me and I am in the Father. (John 10:38)

Be Content

While praying, I felt Jesus take me to an upper room. It was large with wooden floors and little to no furniture. One older sweet-looking lady was sitting while looking out a large glass window into a green lush yard. She was content doing just that. She would sit and watch as the seasons passed by and was content with whatever the season was. When Jesus introduced me, He told me that her name was Ruth.

Ruth was not a lady sitting looking out a window like you might picture at a retirement home. She was peaceful and full of love, life, and joy. As she sat she enjoyed life, not striving to do something, but she truly loved peace.

I (as an adult) walked over and sat down next to her in a chair. We looked out of a huge glass window not talking or feeling the need to fill the quietness with words. We felt truly content and peaceful just sitting and watching others play and laugh as they walked by.

After some time I got up, she smiled and waved goodbye—never the need to talk. I waved and smiled knowing she was not lonely when I left, nor was she disappointed because I did not stay longer. She turned her head continuing to enjoy watching others laugh and play, feeling totally content, lacking nothing.

She was content when I came over; she was content to sit and look out the window and not talk with me; she was content when I left.

The revelation I received was about the world and how it puts pressure on a person to always be busy and doing things, including the pressure to perform. It seems if one is not super busy doing stuff, then they are not successful or valuable to society.

The word "content" means to make satisfied, gratified, and happy.

It Doesn't Matter

On this day I was feeling overlooked because others were promoted. But while worshiping, I felt I was to go visit Ruth, the contented lady in Heaven. As I popped in (which was super easy) she was glad I had decided to come by and said I should come sit and look out the window with her.

Without me saying anything, Ruth said, "That tree isn't angry because that other tree was chosen to do something. It doesn't affect who that tree is. That flower isn't angry because that other one is doing something different. It continues to burst forth with praise to God! That tree continues to burst forth with life and praise even when another tree is chosen to be made into a redwood china closet, or to be a part of a huge redwood house. That doesn't affect who it is!"

I said, "Yea, I know but…" She patted my hand and said, "Yes, but it doesn't change who you are! So remember who you are!" I could see Jesus standing behind me watching us. He was making sure I felt comfortable with Ruth!

Don't forget you are chosen like it states in 1 Peter 2:9 (KJV):

> But ye are a chosen generation, a royal priesthood, an holy nation, a peculiar people; that ye should shew forth the praises of him who hath called you out of darkness into his marvelous light.

Hammock Chair

Jesus and I were sitting in a hammock chair by a beach in Heaven (I was a child). Little kids walked by and gave me flowers and kissed and tickled my hand. Jesus laughed.

This fun intimacy with Jesus is available for everyone who has asked Jesus Christ to be the Lord and Savior of their life. When someone prays to invite Jesus to be their Lord and Savior, it places them in the Father, and in Jesus, and puts Jesus in them. They become one with the Father, Son, and the Holy Spirit.

When we are placed inside of the Father, Son, and Holy Spirit, we can hear Their voice. A spirit of doubt would like to make us think we can't hear, but that is a lie of the enemy. Don't partner with the spirit of doubt and unbelief. Say out loud, "I will not partner with the spirit of doubt and unbelief, but I partner with the Holy Spirit and the Spirit of Truth."

Peace of Mind in My Rock House

Jesus and I sat in my rock house on the hill, in Heaven; it's where we go sometimes. I was an adult on this visit and we sat on a big couch, arm in arm, looking out the huge glass window to watch it snow, while listening to the crackling fire.

Jesus said, "Many, many others have never felt the peace that you feel in your mind. You don't have to do anything for it, but many don't know that. You can rest, but many have never felt that peace and rest. What you are feeling is a blessing that many can't feel because they are so driven to perform and produce. They are works oriented."

Then as we sat and watched the snow fall and pile up, He said, "Each flake is different; it shows my Daddy's creativity. Every flake praises Him. Every flake has a sound of music; the air is full of music." He watched with such joy as it snowed. Nothing satisfies like being with Him.

> You will guard him and keep him in perfect and constant peace whose mind [both its inclination and its character] is stayed on You, because he commits himself to You, leans on You, and hopes confidently in You. So trust in the Lord (commit yourself to Him, lean on Him, hope confidently in Him) forever; for the Lord God is an everlasting Rock [the Rock of Ages]. (Isaiah 26:3-4)

Playing in the Snow

Again, Jesus and I sat on our couch in the rock house (where He meets me in Heaven), and we were watching the snow. I was a teenager this time and when we were outside, we swung and jumped from the swing into deep piles of soft snow. I jumped on Him, pressing Him down and not letting Him move and said, "Make a snow angel." He mumbled through the snow, "I can't move." So I lay on top of Him where I could freely move and made an angel. We laughed so much!

While looking at the imprint, Jesus said, pointing to His stick figure that was pressed down and held under in the snow, "That's you, Kim," and pointing to the movement I made while laying on top of Him. He said, "That's Me! I do what you can't do!"

When people are pressed down and held under, they can't move and do what Jesus wants them to do. Or, if they hold Him down and won't let Him move, He can't do what He wants to do either.

This place in Heaven is so peaceful, quiet, and fun! There is never any pressure to perform or to be something. "He makes me lie down in green pastures (white snow), he leads me by quiet waters (rock house), He restores my soul." (Psalm 23:2)

Fuzzy Slippers Appear

Jesus and I (as a teen) sat in a different house. This one was a log house, and with my feet up on the window sill, I was looking out the front window. He had built a mansion for me but I seem to have more than one house.

White fuzzy slippers appear on my feet that had warmers built in. I was surprised and Jesus laughed and said, "You liked your other ones, so I got you some more. But these stay warm!"

I sat with His arms wrapped around me as we watched kids sledding down a hill. And we laughed. He knows I like to see that.

Jesus said, "You know you don't have to do things to get Me to love you more!" Jesus knows our motives better than we know ourselves.

2013

Spoiled Child

After quieting my mind down and focusing on Jesus, I saw droplets of oil rolling down on a string and dropping in my eyes. It felt as if I was receiving a fresh new anointing to see in the spirit realm and a cleansing of what I have been seeing in the natural. It reminded me to guard what I watch on news programs. I don't need to watch everything they broadcast.

Jesus said, "I am putting ear muffs on you to drown out other voices that are not Me. I'm putting on you special son-sunglasses to narrow your sight to see Me. I want to spoil you; I want to spoil My child with gifts."

We swung on swings and then we ran through fields of flowers.

In the spirit I saw the words "Blue Skies" over my neighbor's house. When I was back in the natural, I told her what I had seen. She said, "Oh my, that's the song I've been singing all day!"

Swinging in a Jungle

During worship I was in the spirit, and Jesus said, "I remember how you liked the monkey bars. Let's climb and swing." I appeared as a teenager.

We swung from limb to limb, like a monkey would in a jungle. The jungle was thick with fresh, vibrant leaves and brightly colored flowers like you would see in Hawaii. The vines we swung from were sturdy but soft and easy to grab.

I could hear monkeys chattering and birds singing. We played for a long time, laughing at the funny moves we made to reach the next vines, kicking our legs and swinging our arms (I had on pants, not a robe or dress). We didn't fly from limb to limb but swung while laughing so much that it was hard to hang onto the vines. When we stopped and rested we were lying on the ground and Jesus said, "I am opening up Heaven to you like never before because it's time!"

I saw clouds going away and then billions of tiny lights falling down and covering me like a mold. He lifted the mold and stood it up. I thought, "That doesn't look like me, it looks like a captain, tall, straight, and bold."

Jesus said, "This is how I see you."

Jesus sees us differently than we see ourselves.

Dancing and Cooking with Jesus

During about three and a half hours of praying and loving on Jesus, I had the following experience: Jesus began to slow dance with me (as an adult). He was teaching me and telling me to "Let it go!"

He said, "It's not your responsibility to raise them up. It's not your responsibility to raise up the church. It's mine!"

Jesus said, "Let it go and relax. Follow My movements; follow and we will become as one dancer. Become one with Me and relax your arms, hips, neck, head, and legs." We danced for an hour as I was learning to let go!

Then we baked cookies in the kitchen in Heaven—sugar cookies with chocolate chips. I looked and people started coming into the kitchen.

My mom appeared and hugged me and said, "I'm sorry we didn't do this more! Listen to Jesus. He gives you little nuggets while He's talking and you don't want to miss them." They laughed.

Jesus said, "Oh, you cook and they'll come," and laughed wholeheartedly!

We danced more in the kitchen and this time I molded to Him quicker. I asked Jesus about being taken to other places supernaturally and helping others.

He said, "Oh, we could set the depressed free, we could push back darkness, and we could heal the sick because there will always be someone who needs those things. But not everyone just wants to stop and be with Me. They want to do, not be! Just be with me now. There's always time to do—but for now, just be!"

Jesus' Garden

Jesus took me to His garden and I appeared as an adult. The garden had an archway of greenery, flowers, and leaves and they all reached out to Him. I put one of my hands in the greenery and it wrapped around my hand. As I leaned into the plants they would wrap around me, tickling me. I began to lie upright against the living archway and stretched out my arms. Again it tickled as it reached out and wrapped around me. Then I rolled over and put my face in it. I could hear Jesus laughing at my new discovery. My face tingled with life. My whole body tingled with life.

I came out of the garden and we walked over to the grass. I just had to lay down in it, on my back. Jesus lay beside me. The grass tickled my armpits with life. I heard Jesus laugh, so I jumped on Him and lifted His arms up so the grass tickled His armpits too. We laughed so much together!

We got up and He said, "Let's go over there." As we walked out of Jesus' garden, I noticed the green railing was alive too, so I sunk my fingers though the greenery to try to feel the wood that I thought was supporting it, but there wasn't any. The thick lush plant itself made the railing and its structure. I pulled a chunk off and saw it was alive in my hands. I asked if I could keep it. He laughed and said, "Oh yes!" I looked up, and we stood at the edge of the most beautiful valley where everything was covered in thick, lush, and very alive greenery.

Jesus said, "My Father is the source of all life; the life comes from the throne."

I was instantly on Daddy's (God's) lap. I put my hands on His face and asked if I could have this power of life to give?"

He said, "You've asked a good thing." But I knew it wasn't the right thing, so I asked, "How can this power get to the people?"

He said, "I am the source. Only I give life, but it can go through your arm to deliver it!" I realized that I never could give power or be the carrier of life, but it's God who gives it through me.

I said, "So you really will listen when I pray for someone?"

He said, "Pray and ask Me this, 'Father what would you like to say to, or do for this person?' Then I will tell you, because it's out of obedience and us moving together that things are accomplished. I am the Giver of the power, and your arm is the avenue. You never could heal or release power in you because you're not the source—I AM!"

> Yet for us there is [only] one God, the Father, Who is the Source of all things and for Whom we [have life], and one Lord, Jesus Christ, through and by Whom are all things and through and by Whom we [ourselves exist]. (1 Corinthians 8:6)

Jesus' Blue Room

While I was worshiping Jesus, He took me to His Blue Room where there is no gravity (which is funny since He can fly anyway), but He likes it. I was a teenager and we were floating. I saw that the room was made of tiny blue tiles. I looked at one and could see through it for years in advance. I saw Italy the way it will be in the years after Jesus restores it.

He said, "Every city, state, and county are in these blue tiles. They are portals and you can go anywhere at any time. These are portals to everywhere, if you have the faith to go. They are there with everyone you meet. You can travel through their portals and see their lives because they are all already open. People are praying for portals to open when they are *already* open."

I could see this huge room was covered in these tiny tiles. And they were so easy to travel through; they almost pulled you in. It is very, very easy to travel through someone's life to somewhere in time.

Relationship Makes Fruit

During worship, I felt my spirit ascend and look back at me. Instantly I was flying (as an adult), with Jesus flying beside me. He said, "You've been flying with Me for over twenty years now. Don't get it in your head that it's hard. There is no distance in time so you can go here and there, back and forth in time when ministering to someone. That is called getting Words of Wisdom and Words of Knowledge. And that comes from a relationship with Me combined with faith—together producing fruit. You've been seeking the fruit but what you are really looking for is the relationship with Me that produces the fruit!"

Jesus Dunked Me

Jesus and I played in a waterfall. He dunked me and I dunked Him. Jesus only has eyes for me and loves to play and swim with me. When you are with Him, it will be the same for you. Vacations with Jesus are the best!

The Scroll

I sat at a table with Daddy, Jesus, and the Holy Spirit. Daddy unrolled my scroll and began to read it. Instantly I was reminded of the scroll Jesus read in Luke 4:16 (MSG):

> When he stood up to read, he was handed the scroll of the prophet Isaiah. Unrolling the scroll, he found the place where it was written, God's Spirit is on me; he's chosen me to preach the Message of good news to the poor, Sent me

to announce pardon to prisoners and recovery of sight to the blind, To set the burdened and battered free, to announce, "This is God's time to shine." (or "This is God's year to act!") He rolled up the scroll, handed it back to the assistant, and sat down. Every eye in the place was on him, intent. Then he started in, "You've just heard Scripture make history. It came true just now in this place."

Then Daddy said to me, "When I formed you, I reached and placed stars in your eyes to shine. I put a piece of My heart in you so you would never feel unloved or second best. I gathered the warmth from the sun, the streams, and the waterfalls, and placed them in you. I watched you play at my feet and dance with others. As you grew you heard the cries and you ran to the edge to look over. As you grew more, the cries from their hearts grew louder and you ran to see. You began to cry and ask Me, 'Why do they cry, Daddy? Why are they hurting and so sad?'"

He said, "That's when I knew what pulled on you. I let you go to the hurting hearts. You've tried to heal the sick when actually, 'healing the hearts' is your call." I felt light and heat cover my eyes to burn up the sin of striving to heal the sick, rather than having peace to heal the hearts.

Hidden in Him

I saw Jesus riding a horse and He had on this long robe covered in jewels. When I saw it, all I could say is, "Your Majesty! Your Majesty!" (see Revelation 5:12).

Jesus lifted me up and put me on the back of the horse, and then pulled me inside of Him—I was hidden in Him. Where He went, I went. I was in Him as people worshiped Him; it was so cool. I was hidden in Him just like it says in scripture:

> For you died, and your life is now hidden with Christ in God. (Colossians 3:3 NIV)
>
> Saying in a loud voice, Deserving is the Lamb, Who was sacrificed, to receive all the power and riches and wisdom and might and honor and majesty (glory, splendor) and blessing! (Revelation 5:12)

Leap Time and Space

During worship I saw Jesus and I was a teen. He said, "Do you want to go somewhere?"

I said, "Yes!" We stood on an edge and jumped off, holding hands. But instead of falling, we flew.

Jesus said, "I can leap time," and I could feel we jumped through time and space.

He said, "This is one of the planets that is light-years away." I saw lots of twirly living things. We stood at an opening looking out to the atmosphere.

I heard, "Throw and create," so I threw balls of colors and straight flashes of light.

He said, "This is your galaxy. This will always exist!"

Then I stood on what felt like glass, it was smooth but not slick. I looked down and although it looked like marble, it changed colors. The colors were like a pretty, smoky substance that continually changed under my feet. The plants also changed colors.

Jesus said, "Here everything changes color constantly. It's called, 'The Color Planet.'" I lay down with my face to the ground and watched it change colors. Jesus laughed at my joy of watching the ground change colors.

I Can Smell Him

I sat on Daddy's lap in our garden and He showed me how He was whittling an image of Himself, for me. He said, "I know how you like pictures of the ones you love!" (I was a child and an adult on this visit.)

Then I saw a field of butterflies—they were everywhere! We held hands and He became (what seemed like to me) two stories tall!

I said, "But I can always reach your hand!" We ran through the butterflies. They flew to my arms and began to change colors and of course, they sang or made music.

Peal (my horse) came up to me and I got on. I asked if Daddy wanted to ride, and He got on behind me, put His arms around me, and held onto the reins. I began crying because riding my horse with Daddy in a field of butterflies was truly amazing. I noticed that many spots in my heart were healed. This experience filled the hurt and the void.

Daddy looked in my eyes and said, "I want you whole and I can make you whole in every place that is void!" Jesus came up and Daddy was gone.

Jesus bent down to me then He stood up with His ams wide open, with His head back, sniffing the air and saying, "I can smell Him; I can smell My Father!"

I realized I was now *in* Jesus and then suddenly I could smell fresh rain. Jesus said, "There's nothing more important than smelling My Father! He's coming. I can smell Him. There's no place to jump to or finger to move. There's nothing more important than smelling My father— He's coming!

You know how when you have an unexpected guest suddenly arrive, you jump up to clean the house? Well, Jesus was saying there was no need to jump and clean, or even lift a finger to do anything when you're visiting with God—JUST BE! There is no action or work more important than just being in His presence and smelling Him.

I saw a thick fog rolling down the field. While in Him, I said this together with Jesus, "Everything in Me wants to be filled: every cell in my body calls out to You. Every hair and every cell in every strand calls out to You; every tooth calls out to You (weird, I know)." I could feel God overshadowing Jesus and me. I was in Jesus but I could feel Daddy.

Jesus said, "Nothing—no act, no movement of any kind is more valuable than being with My Father!"

This encounter felt like only ten or fifteen minutes, but it was actually one and a half hours later that it lifted and I was back on the earth.

> "The one who has spoken these things says, 'I am coming soon!' So, Lord Jesus, please come soon!" (Revelation 22:20 CEV)

2014–2015

Swimming with Jesus

After a few minutes of worshiping, I was instantly in Heaven as a child. It has become as easy as walking into another room for me.

Jesus and I hugged and ran down a grassy hill. We jumped into a pool-like place and floated on top of huge colorful beach balls.

I said, "I have missed you!"

He said, "I've missed you too." Then with His hand He hit my ball right out from under me and laughed. When I came up, I jumped on Him and dunked Him. Then we dunked each other and laughed and played. After playing for a while, we floated on our backs enjoying just being together again.

Lots of Bubbles

I was worshiping when I saw a huge soap bubble where the colors on it swirled and changed. On this visit I was a child, and a teen.

Jesus said, "Change: Where there's life, there's change. Life brings change and change is good!"

Daddy God said, "See the colored bubbles." Instantly I began to see bubbles of all colors. As I ran into them they covered me and the bubbles became jewels on a robe. The robe had long sleeves and a train. Everything was covered in elongated colorful jewels; they used to be bubbles but had turned into these five-plus inches long jewels! This reminded me of Isaiah 61:10 "... and as a bride adorns herself with her jewels."

Jesus said, "The jewels represent your various characteristics. You are gentle, compassionate, patient, loving, forgiving, and tender.... This is how I see you!" Jesus sees us differently than we see ourselves, and He sees others differently than we see them.

Jesus said, "You are rewarded here in Heaven for what you do on earth. Here I acknowledge you and reward you. On earth, affirmations or rewards are forgotten in a short time. But here in Heaven, those who bless others are acknowledged for all of eternity!"

Once again I saw beautiful colors like the Northern Lights. The best way to describe the swirling colors is the feeling you might have standing inside a bubble.

I said to Jesus, "I feel like I'm in a soap bubble." I saw Jesus tossing around a huge colorful bubble and there were also other people playing there. Doesn't scripture say in Matthew 18:3 to become like little children? Then He lightly tossed the bubble to me and we tossed it back and forth. I had to be careful because it was like tossing a huge water balloon. It was fun.

And then I said, "Why do you always show me fun things? I want to work. I want to cast out devils and stuff!"

Jesus said, "Here, there are no worries about things. There is no heaviness and there are no concerns. Heaven is light and happy. When people go to Loco Motion (a kid's fun place) they say, 'OK, we are here to have fun for a few hours and not worry about bills, and so on.' It is the same here; we don't worry, we have fun!"

> I delight greatly in the Lord; my soul rejoices in my God. For he has clothed me with garments of salvation and arrayed me in a robe of his righteousness, as a bridegroom adorns his head like a priest, and as a bride adorns herself with her jewels. (Isaiah 61:10 NIV)

> And said, Truly I say to you, unless you turn about and become like little children [trusting, lowly, loving, forgiving], you can never enter the kingdom of Heaven [at all]. (Matthew 18:3)

Breathe in Life

I was standing in a river in Heaven and I could hear a waterfall above me. I turned my face upward and breathed in the water falling down around me. It felt like I was breathing in gemstones. I stood in the river, stuck my face in the water, and just breathed in! Somehow I knew I could do this and not get choked. I scooped up handfuls of water and breathed them in. Jesus stood and laughed with me. I took His hair and breathed it in! I could breathe in His hair!

Instantly, we were standing in the grass, so I took handfuls of grass and leaves and flowers and I could also breathe them in. They are all full of life and can be breathed in. Jesus stood holding my hand and He breathed in the air of Heaven. And I did too. The air of Heaven that we were breathing in appeared as tiny diamond dew drops.

He said, "Breathe in, then blow out. Take it in, and then give it out! This reminded me of scriptures that tell us about the breath of life.

> ...breathed into His nostrils the breath of Life (Genesis 2:7)

> ...and with that He breathed on them and said, "Receive the Holy Spirit" (John 20:22)

Jesus' Ice Skates

During worship I saw Jesus on ice skates. I had on a beautiful royal robe and skates! We danced and skated together; we flowed simultaneously with each other and I could see His face clearer than normal.

> By the breath of God ice is given, and the breadth of the waters is frozen over. (Job 37:10)

> He casts forth His ice like crumbs; who can stand before His cold? (Psalm 147:17)

Heaven is Real and Fun

Chapter 2

Daddy God and the Holy Spirit in Heaven

He wants us to draw near to Him and to know Him

> But as for me, it is good for me to draw near to God; I have made the Lord God my refuge and placed my trust in Him, That I may tell of all Your works. (Psalm 73:28)

He sees us every day and thinks about us

> How precious also are Your thoughts to me, O God! How vast is the sum of them! If I could count them, they would outnumber the sand. When I awake, I am still with You. (Psalm139:17–18)

He wants us to know Him

> Now this is eternal life: that they may know You, the only true [supreme and sovereign] God, and [in the same manner know] Jesus [as the] Christ whom You have sent. (John 17:3)

My prayer is not for them alone. I pray also for those who will believe in me through their message, that all of them may be one, Father, just as you are in me and I am in you. May they also be in us so that the world may believe that you have sent me. I have given them the glory that you gave me, that they may be one as we are one—I in them and you in me—so that they may be brought to complete unity. Then the world will know that you sent me and have loved them even as you have loved me. Father, I want those you have given me to be with me where I am, and to see my glory, the glory you have given me because you loved me before the creation of the world. Righteous Father, though the world does not know you, I know you, and they know that you have sent me. I have made you[a] known to them, and will continue to make you known in order that the love you have for me may be in them and that I myself may be in them. (John 17: 20-26 NIV)

He wants us

Therefore, believers, since we have confidence and full freedom to enter the Holy Place [the place where God dwells] by [means of] the blood of Jesus, by this new and living way which He initiated and opened for us through the veil [as in the Holy of Holies], that is, through His flesh, and since we have a great and wonderful Priest [Who rules] over the house of God, let us approach [God] with a true and sincere heart in unqualified assurance of faith, having had our hearts sprinkled clean from an evil conscience and our bodies washed with pure water. (Hebrews 10:19–22)

2000–2011

The Storehouse of Elements

I had been worshiping, and suddenly the Holy Spirit took me to the Storehouse of Elements. An angel and I (as an adult) began walking down a hallway, looking through large square glass rooms with no floors or ceilings.

The first room I looked in had shafts or beams of light shining down. Some of the beams were thin and some were wide. They looked like spotlights beaming down.

The next three rooms we walked by had bolts of lightning (see Exodus 9:22–24, Psalm 77:17, Revelation 11:18–19). The first room had skinny bolts of lightning. The next two rooms had very large bolts of lightning. There wasn't a floor or walls in any of the rooms so the lightning seemed to go way down.

The angel said, "Shafts of light are just to prepare them (people on earth) for the next phase. The lightning will come from the hands of people who will strike others." I understood he meant that when someone is ministering to a person and they reach their hand out toward them, it is as if lightning is flowing through the ministering person's hands, touching the other one. This is a good thing that demonstrates the power of God and brings a good change in the person.

Then as we continued down the hallway, I saw a room with whirlwinds of different sizes and strengths (see Psalm 77:17).

The angel said, "People (on earth) will experience feelings like a whirling around them and some will actually be taken and translated physically to other locations." My body started jerking and twirling with the lightning and the whirlwinds.

The angel reached over and said, "Receive a body that can handle the things of the spirit." After that, nothing seemed to affect my body.

We walked on. There was a room where it rained and rained, never seeming to stop. And there was a room with different-sized clouds. Some clouds were cute and small, like little puffs; some were larger. Then we walked further and saw a room full of rainbows of all different sizes and types.

Then in the next room I saw hail. The hailstones were huge, round, hard, and smooth; they were the size of large coconuts or bowling balls (see Revelation 11:18–19). The angel seemed sad, but not sad at just this room, but at the next room also. In this next room it was snowing, seeming to never stop.

I asked, "What does this hallway mean?"

He said, "The first rooms are God's provisions: shafts of light, lightning, rain (cleansing from hurts and refreshing), and clouds (carrying peace and healing). The second group of rooms are God's promises: whirlwinds and rainbows. The third group are God's judgements: hail and snow."

I asked, "How do the rainbows work?"

He said, "People may be sitting in a conference and will suddenly see a rainbow going from one person to another. That will be the person God has sent to bring the promise God told them about. For example: One will need finances at one end of the rainbow; a person at the other end will have the finances to give, and God will bring them together."

"One will be searching for a mate and at the other end of the rainbow is the promised mate. One will need a place to stay and on the other end of a rainbow, the person has a spare room. One may need a ride and on the other end of a rainbow there is a person who can provide. One end of a rainbow may go from one person and then other end would go to the Father. That means He hasn't forgotten His promise to them, and He will provide."

He said, "No man can manifest these things. No man can manifest light from His hands, or clouds in a room that will carry peace and healings. No man can manifest rain to fall in a room for the cleansing of sin and hurts, and then bring a refreshing."

He continued. "The hail will come in towns where they have not experienced it, and so they are not prepared. The snow is beautiful until it doesn't quit. Go tell about this hallway. It doesn't matter if they believe it or not. God has allowed only a few to see this Storehouse of Elements!"

> Then Moses stretched forth his rod toward the Heavens, and the Lord sent thunder and hail, and fire (lightning) ran down to and along the ground, and the Lord rained hail upon the land of Egypt. (Exodus 9:22–24)

Have you entered the treasuries of the snow, or have you seen the treasuries of the hail, Which I have reserved for the time of trouble, for the day of battle and war? (Job 38:22-23)

The voice of Your thunder was in the whirlwind, the lightning's illumined the world; the earth trembled and shook. (Psalm 77:18)

Then the sanctuary of God in Heaven was thrown open, and the ark of His covenant was seen standing inside in His sanctuary; and there were flashes of lightning, loud rumblings (blasts, mutterings), peals of thunder, an earthquake, and a terrific hailstorm. (Revelation 11:19

God's Not Good – He's Magnificent!

I had been worshiping when I was caught up into Heaven as an adult. Daddy God stood before me. I began telling God how good He is.

And He said, "I'm not only good; I am magnificent, powerful, awesome, and full of every good thing. I am glorious and amazing. I have all the answers to every situation. I have every direction for every question. I know all. I am as amazing today as I was yesterday, and I will be just as amazing tomorrow. No one can move Me from this amazing place. No one can move Me from this throne; no one can vote Me off and no one can vote Me out! It's like an ant under your toe, trying to move you from your chair; it won't happen. It can't be done. Neither can anyone move Me! Come into My amazing presence."

I could feel the strong rumbling under my feet that surrounded me like a mighty waterfall! He is so amazing!

He said, "There is nothing too hard for Me to fix. What kind of Creator would create a world that was too hard for Him to fix? I am your High Tower, your Shield, your Helmet, your Breastplate, your Belt, and your Shoes. I am the covering for your lips, like lipstick."

He covered my mouth so I was able to speak right. "I am the covering for your eyes, like eye shadow, so you can see the good in people. I am the covering for your ears, like earrings, so you can hear the good. I am your purse; everything you need is found in Me!"

God said, "I am so in love with you; I think you are beautiful to watch. I think you are wonderful to be with. I am your God, your best friend, and I have great plans that will come to you; plans that are greater than you know. I AM amazing! Come into my amazing presence and receive from Me amazing revelations!"

> The Lord is my Rock, my Fortress, and my Deliverer; my God, my keen and firm Strength in Whom I will trust and take refuge, my Shield, and the Horn of my salvation, my High Tower. (Psalm 18:2)

Ascending Is a Tool

I was caught up during worship, into Heaven and Daddy God said, "Ascending into Heaven is a tool. It's not some super-spiritual thing any more than is fasting, speaking, or binding demons. It's a tool. Come get My wisdom."

This event reminded me of Jesus telling John to "Come up here" in Revelation 4:1.

> After this I looked, and behold, a door standing open in Heaven! And the first voice which I had heard addressing

me like a war trumpet said, Come up here, and I will show you what must take place in the future.

My Father Is an Artist

During worship I saw a ladder almost like a rope ladder. But I didn't need it, I just floated up past it. Jesus hugged me as soon as I saw Him and said, "I want to introduce you to someone."

We turned and Jesus said, "Here are Abraham and Joshua. You've already met Ruth (Boaz's wife)." I had met Ruth on a previous visit, she was very loving and approachable, she wore traditional clothes.

Jesus introduced me, "This is Kim," and they shook my hand and said, "We've heard about you!"

Then Jesus and I went and sat on a white, two-person bench and a movie screen appeared. Jesus said, "Here, would you like some grapes? (They just instantly appeared). I know you like these chocolate-covered grapes!" I took some and began to eat. They had the texture and shape of a grape but not the taste, and were covered in the best chocolate! The closest chocolate to it that I have tasted, was made in Switzerland.

Jesus showed me how He and our Father created the earth.

Jesus said, "When God My Father moves, life appears. He would move His finger and instantly flowers grew, and colors burst forth."

Jesus said, "You have an artist as a Father. My Father is an artist! As He spoke, grass, vines, flowers, trees (thick and colorful) would appear; water became full of living things and the sky filled with living things."

Jesus said, "We love life! We love living things! Even the air is full of life! The rocks and even the dirt are full of life! Father loves life. He creates life. I am opening your eyes to see life. If something is not filled with life, then it's not of My Father. You'll see." He waved bye and promised, "I'll see you!"

As I began to float back to my prayer room, I saw big colorful birds and animals playing with each other and Jesus said, "We laugh when we watch them play, just as you do!"

> My help will come from the Lord, the Creator of Heaven and earth. (Psalm 121:2 ERV)

Petals of Favor

I felt such a drawing to the spirit realm tonight. During prayer, I stepped over into the spirit realm and I stood, as a teenager, and saw colorful flower petals falling down. As they began to fill up the floor, I scooped them up and threw them in the air. They were thick and so soft. As they came down they all sang or had musical sounds coming from each one.

Jesus said, "Walk around and go down the stairs." (Instantly a set of stairs appeared.) "Go deeper!" I began to walk down the stairs and it began to fill up with flower petals.

I asked (in thought), "What do the petals mean?" and I heard, "It's the favor of God."

I heard Daddy God say, "It's My favor. You have great favor from Me. Keep walking!" As I did, the petals grew so numerous that they reached over my head. I stretched up my arm and couldn't reach through them; they were so deep.

He said, "Jump" so I jumped up and still couldn't reach out through them.

My Daddy said, "You can't outreach My favor. Now run!" I ran and the petals were always there, and deep.

He said, "Turn around and run back," and it was just as thick and deep.

Daddy said, "You can't outrun My favor! Now ask what you will, and I will do it for you!"

> The grace (blessing and favor) of the Lord Jesus Christ be with all the saints (God's holy people, those set apart for God, to be, as it were, exclusively His). Amen! (Revelation 22:21 AMPC)

I Would Look over the Edge

During worship, I was instantly in Heaven standing beside Daddy God as a child.

He was sitting on a fancy chair and said, "I knew you before you were born (see Jeremiah 1:5). You would look over the edge of the creation balcony and see the sick and say to Me, 'Father let me go; I will teach them healing, and I will teach them about Jesus. They don't have to be that way. I will teach them. Let me go.'

And I said to you, 'Some will not listen.'

And you said to Me, 'But some will, Daddy, some will listen. They don't have to be sick because of your love, because of what Jesus did for them. They don't have body parts, but you can give them parts and heal them. Let me go!'"

Daddy said, "I blessed you, Kim, and I breathed into you My life and sent you to teach healing to the small and great—to a few and to many (see Isaiah 61:1). I sent you to teach healing. You wanted to go and teach, so I blessed you and put you into a family. You are not called; you're sent to teach healing. I knew you before you were created in your mother's womb. You were seated with Me in Heavenly places."

> Before I formed you in the womb I knew [and] approved of you [as My chosen instrument], and before you were born I separated and set you apart, consecrating you; [and] I appointed you as a prophet to the nations. (Jeremiah 1:5)

> The Spirit of the Lord God is upon me, because the Lord has anointed and qualified me to preach the Gospel of good tidings to the meek, the poor, and afflicted; He has sent me to bind up and heal the brokenhearted, to proclaim liberty to the [physical and spiritual] captives and the opening of the prison and of the eyes to those who are bound. (Isaiah 61:1)

Let It Go

During worship at church I felt a white whirlwind around me, going upward (see Ps 77:18). I was instantly in the Throne room, as an adult, and I saw people in white robes dancing and worshiping freely (see Revelation 7:9). Daddy said, "There's no heaviness here. Let it go. Let the burden of what to have for lunch go, let it go." He knows our smallest thoughts and what burdens us.

I watched the people freely twirl and dance, and the love from God went into them, filling them with so much love they just felt like bursting with love for God. Out of their fullness of love for God they were worshiping Him, each one saying and singing back to God out of that fullness of love. His love for them would enter them, then their love for Him went back to Him. It went back and forth.

> After this I looked and a vast host appeared which no one could count, [gathered out] of every nation, from all tribes and peoples and languages. These stood before the throne and before the Lamb; they were attired in white robes, with palm branches in their hands. (Revelation 7:9)

The Light Room

During worship I stepped over into the spirit realm, I was an adult on this visit. Jesus and I were sitting on an edge of something that seemed to be made of glass, dangling our feet over the edge like we do on the cliffs. I looked over and saw stars and blackness. We were somewhere higher in the atmosphere, just sitting and looking out.

Jesus laughed and said, "Want me to say, 'Jump'?" I didn't respond. He lay back on the black glass-like substance and put His arm under His head. After a moment Jesus sat up and said, "Kim, all of this you have been given authority over."

I asked, "Have all your children been given this?"

Jesus said, "Only those who can be trusted."

Then He leaned back and said while looking up, "This is all for My Father. He is so worth it all. He is worth it all!"

We were instantly standing in front of our Daddy, bowing down. The love and power that radiated from Him was awesome. God said, "There is a door you may walk through which leads you to teach and lead individuals to Me. Through this door are miracles never before seen on earth." I saw a door open and Jesus was on the other side. I ran and jumped into Jesus' arms, and He laughed with me.

God said, "This is a door; it is not you doing anything, but it's a door being opened so you may speak and lead people to Me. Your life will never, ever be the same. When you go into hotels, people will be delivered and healed."

I saw myself saying to the cripple, "Be as you should be; time has been broken." I saw the dead come to life and then heard them speak of seeing Jesus.

God said, "There is a door, and it has nothing to do with your ability!"

Later I saw a brightly lit room and He said, "Walk into it!" I walked in and heard myself say, "See through me, examine my mind, eyes, stomach, legs, feet, arms, hands, motives, and so forth."

God said, "I call this the Light Room." He laughed and said, "Nothing is hidden from Me. Come here often."

Please examine the following passage. Nothing is hidden from Him: He knows about everyone, everywhere.

> Everything about us is bare and wide open to the all-seeing eyes of our living God; nothing can be hidden from him to whom we must explain all that we have done. (Hebrews 4:13 TLB)

God's Fog Machine

As a teenager, I saw God sitting on His throne. It was bright and white and yellowish. There was a thick cloud around the floor; you could scoop it up but you couldn't feel it. The phrase from Isaiah 6:1 declaring "His train filled the temple" came to mind. It looked as if the substance came from His robe, then flowed down and out to the floor.

Daddy said, "You have fog machines that are sort of like this, but you can't make this consistency," and He laughed.

He said, "I'll wrap you in My glory." He proceeded to pick it up and then wrap it around me like a safety barrier and said, "It is our secret place!" Then Jesus walked in and sat with me in the glory. It was like a teepee of bright-light glory.

> In the year that King Uzziah died, [in a vision] I saw the Lord sitting upon a throne, high and lifted up, and the skirts of His train filled the temple. (Isaiah 6:1)

God Loves the Smell of Worship

During worship Jesus said, "Let me give you a revelation of My Father." We walked into the throne room and God was inhaling fragrances (see 2 Corinthians 2:15).

Jesus said, "He loves the fragrance that flowers give. Worship, sacrifice, and purity give off a fragrance like flowers."

> For we are the sweet fragrance of Christ [which exhales] unto God, [discernible alike] among those who are being saved and among those who are perishing. (2 Corinthians 2:15)

Holy Spirit Baton

The Holy Spirit appeared to me. I was an adult and He was a tall, strong person with blond, almost-white, long hair and said, "I am giving you the baton to run the next leg of the race. Will you take it? You have been given authority. Now stand up straight, put your shoulders back, hold your head up, and walk in it."

As He handed me a baton, it felt heavy in my hands (see 1 Corinthians 9:24). I then had the sensation that something heavy was being lifted off of my back, while at the same time something like a heavy blanket was resting on and covering my shoulders.

> You know that in a race all the runners run, but only one runner gets the prize. So run like that. Run to win! (1 Corinthians 9:24 ERV)

2012

Daddy Smells like Love, Openness, and Rain

I was a child and an adult on this visit. My age changes in Heaven and I have no control over that. I heard and saw Jesus, and I also saw a group of people. They began to hug me and say, "We are proud of you." It was a great feeling to be acknowledged for not giving up and not giving in to the pressures of life!

Then I told Daddy I wanted to smell Him. My Daddy has a smell of love (see 2 Corinthians 2:14-16) and I desired to smell Him. I began to open up my heart and spirit. I could smell openness, and I could smell the scent of rain. I turned and ran, and jumped onto Daddy's lap. He wrapped His arms around me and I asked, "May I smell you?" I buried my face in His neck.

He said, "Yield, relax, and yield more. I am moving, and you need to yield like the soft plant in the front yard, and have a tender un-bitter heart (see Ezekiel 11:19). A bitter heart will cause hardness like a tree, and it doesn't yield to the flowing wind."

> And I will give them one heart [a new heart] and I will put a new spirit within them; and I will take the stony

[unnaturally hardened] heart out of their flesh, and will give them a heart of flesh [sensitive and responsive to the touch of their God]. (Ezekiel 11:19)

But thanks be to God! For through what Christ has done, he has triumphed over us so that now wherever we go he uses us to tell others about the Lord and to spread the Gospel like a sweet perfume. As far as God is concerned there is a sweet, wholesome fragrance in our lives. It is the fragrance of Christ within us, an aroma to both the saved and the unsaved all around us. To those who are not being saved, we seem a fearful smell of death and doom, while to those who know Christ we are a life-giving perfume. But who is adequate for such a task as this? (2 Corinthians 2:14–16 TLB)

Daddy Said, "I Know All"

Jesus took me to a balcony overlooking an ocean.

I heard Daddy say, "I know how many creatures and what species live in there. I know of the ones that haven't been discovered yet. I know how many grains of sand are on that beach. It's irrelevant, but I do know! I know all!"

There is no need to fear the future because Daddy knows all. Like the scriptures say in Psalm 139 and like 1 John tells us:

There is no fear in love; but perfect love casteth out fear: because fear hath torment. He that feareth is not made perfect in love. (1 John 4:18 KJV)

Flying around the Throne

During worship I said to Jesus, "I want to go deeper." I saw a shallow pool with a cement bottom. Jesus and I as an adult, held hands and began walking into the water. Then we just went through the bottom like it wasn't there and continued down deeper into the pool.

An angel said, "You have asked the Father to see Him (see Matthew 5:8) and He will do what you have requested. Will you trust me?" I said, "Yes," and He took my hand. We flew around the throne room in huge circles passing through rows of rainbow colors, worshiping the Father, listening, and watching others worship the Father!

The angel seemed to be wearing a long white robe and looked human-like (not like a weird creature with three heads). In Heaven you can fly without wings, so this angel may have had wings, I don't know, but all I could focus on was God, His pureness, the people and the colors. The angel seemed almost irrelevant at the time but I was comforted knowing he knew it was okay for me to be flying with him around the Father.

As I flew around the throne, holding hands with the angel, I could see a characteristic or aspect of God appear like the flicker of light off a diamond. Each sparkle or flicker would reveal the pureness of God: And that one characteristic was so incredibly pure that the only thing I could say was, "HOLY" before another flicker of God would spark yet another pure characteristic of God—and I could again only say, "HOLY" before yet another flicker of God's pureness was revealed.

When I am impressed, I might say "holy cow," but Father's pureness was so overwhelming and came so quickly that I couldn't get out, "cow," just "HOLY!" At times as I was flying around the throne, I couldn't even get the word "HOLY" out, just a "H…"

Now I see why the angels fly around the throne and say nothing but HOLY! His love was being revealed at such a deep, pure, clean, nothing-dark, absolutely pure level, that all you could say was, "HOLY!"

Then the joy of God would be revealed as so pure, deep, clean, with no bitterness, no hiding, just a totally pure joy that all you could say was "HOLY!" Then another flicker would be the grace of God, then His love for children, then His heart for animals. Everything for all of eternity is revealed at the throne that all you can say is "HOLY" – not even "cow."

I saw Father sitting on His throne as people in the throne room danced, bowed, and laid their crowns at his feet. And I could see His pure joy and love in what He was seeing. Total pure love for his children with no hidden bitterness towards them. Only pure and total love for them! And all I could say as I watched Him observing the people was, "HOLY!"

God wore a white robe type of garment and His hair, long and white, glowed. The rainbow colors flowed around and out of Him as we flew through them and on them. Nothing mattered except Him and seeing what pure love, pure acceptance, and pure joy really looked like.

God is really NICE and so PURE.

Matthew 5:8 says, "Blessed are the pure in heart, for they will see God."

Waterfall Swing

During worship the Holy Spirit showed me a group of children, maybe from Africa, and He said, "Pray for mothers for these orphans!" (I was a teen.)

Then Jesus took my hand and we walked behind a waterfall. He pushed me on a swing that went through the waterfall and I swung out past the waterfall on the other side of it. We were swinging high above the water where I could jump off into the deep pool below, come up, swim over to the bank, and do it again.

Jesus said, "I know your eyes are on Me, and your mind is set on Heavenly things, and on eternity and eternal things. Nothing on earth satisfies you. I've spoiled you, showing you the best things and giving you the best things. I have spoiled my bride, the one I love, the most important person in My life!"

I Saw the Holy Spirit

During worship I began to pray and I said, "Holy Spirit, I want to be introduced to you."

Jesus and I, as an adult, were instantly in Heaven, and Jesus said, "Here is the Holy Spirit." I looked to my left and there stood a tall, muscular being with long, blond (almost-white) hair.

He said, "Hi," and I ran and jumped into His arms and threw my arms around His neck while saying, "May I jump into your arms like I do to Jesus, and can I hug You the way I hug Jesus?" He hugged me and laughed. Then I passed through Him even though He had a form.

I stood holding His hand in my left hand, and the Father held His, and Jesus held the Father's and mine. The four of us formed a circle holding hands. Jesus said, "You always wanted to be a part of the crowd!" They laughed and began to walk through each other, changing places but still holding my hand. They walked through me and out the other side, still holding hands and forming a circle and laughing.

They said, "Here is something for you," and they made a bubbling fountain in the middle of the circle. I walked into it, and it went into me! I could feel the fountain flowing up inside of me.

I asked the Holy Spirit, "May I go with you and see what you like to do? I bet you like to break things!"

He laughed and said, "Yes, I do like to break and destroy things!" He put His hands over my eyes and said, "You will see Me as you have never seen Me!" I could see bright yellow lights and my eyes felt warm.

He said, "I am Spirit. Everything about Me is Spirit. I didn't come in the flesh like Jesus. Fasting will cause your spirit to be closer to Me, as I am Spirit. I know that's tough, but you will link up with Me!" To me the Holy Spirit is tall and blond, broad and strong. And even though He is a Spirit, He seems more established, stable, and firm than a flesh body does—yet He is so different!

2013

God's Rose Garden

I began to worship and pray in tongues, and almost instantly I was sitting on a park bench, as a child, with Daddy God sitting to my right. He had the form of a man sitting by me. The greenery over our heads began to grow like a thick luscious canopy. Birds, peacocks, and other kinds of animals walked calmly by. I bent down and He handed me a big, fat, soft rabbit to hold. He laughed as He hugged and squeezed me and said, "I'm so glad my children are coming here to see Me!"

He said, "Come! I want to show you something," and He took my hand. He was a tall man with strength but also had a kindness about Him, like Hoss in the show Bonanza. And He's gentle like the dad in that show. We entered a path and went into a rose garden. As I walked, roses began to grow. They were so thick and they quickly carpeted the entire hillside! It happened so *fast,* like someone was rolling out paper! They were roses but the stems were short and thick, and there were all kinds of colors—but mainly red, because I like red.

Daddy said, "This happens because where you walk, it brings great life."

I said, "It's where *You* walk!" He laughed and walked through me.

He said, "I'm in you and you are in Me! It's where *you* walk that brings great life! You're now in My rose garden, so the life in you produces the roses." I waved my arm, and rose petals filled the air. I ran with my arms out, and rose petals poured from the ripples of wind I made. I kicked up my foot and rose petals flew out into the air. I twirled around and the ripples made petals fly from me.

He laughed so much and said, "You've heard of rose water?" Then I saw a spring with clear deep pink rose-colored water flowing from it.

He said, "Where did they get the idea?" and laughed. I put my feet into the water and it was so soft and smelled so good. I got into the water and it ran through me!

I was surprised at how it felt, and He said, "Let it wash away the anger and sadness." I splashed and kicked while rose petals floated out of the water drops that I splashed.

I got out and said, "I proclaim rose petals on the earth: to my church, to my town, and to my prayer room." I felt a huge rush of wind blow by and keep blowing.

Daddy said, "You're in My rose garden and the life here produces roses! Meet me here again, and I'll show you more things!"

> Then the Lord God planted a garden in the east, in a place called Eden [related to a word meaning "luxurious"], and put the man he had formed into it. (Genesis 2:8 EXB)

Clover Crown

Daddy God picked me up and hugged, hugged, hugged me! He made a clover crown with tails like I used to do as a child and put it on my head and said, "You are my princess!" This reminds me of being called a princess in (Psalm 45:13 EXB), "The princess [daughter of the king] is very beautiful [all glorious within]. Her gown is woven with gold."

Mud Castles with Daddy God

I saw Daddy God as if I were a small child and I ran, jumped, and hugged His neck and kissed Him, telling Him how much I missed Him. He laughed and hugged me with both arms.

We walked a little until I sat down and began playing with a stick in a mud puddle. He sat with me. I told Him I was sad about my sister-in-law passing away, which He already knew, of course.

We talked about a healing ministry and how it would take time away from Him, and I so love and value this time. Then He took His hand and made a mud mountain about four inches high. Then He took His fingers and rubbed them together, and it snowed over His mud mountain!

I tried doing that over my mud mountain, and nothing! Ugh! Daddy took my hand, held out His hand, and put my hand inside of His. They were see-through and I could see my hand was inside of His. Then He took His other hand and put it inside my other hand (see Psalm 143:9 and John 10:30). Jesus walked up and smiled and put His hand inside of my hand and inside of Daddy's hand. I could see all three different hands, but we were one body. We were transparent. We were one, but with three different hands. It was so cool!

I leaned back and sank into Daddy and then Jesus walked into us. I could see and feel all three of us, but we were in one body. I got up and sat on a swing, and all three of us swung. We walked. We swung. It's like I had a transparent covering. Daddy said, "When you're alone, praying is hard, right? But when we are one, everything is easier." I could feel the swing, yet I was sitting in Daddy with Jesus. We three were swinging.

We went back to the mud puddle. While sitting there, I was inside Daddy and Jesus. I reached out and could see the three different layers. This time I formed a water fountain out of the mud puddle. It was about four inches high and water flowed up and out. When I stretched out my hand, their hands were stretching out with me. *As long as we were one and I was not doing it alone, it was easy to create.*

This reminds me of the story when Jesus took mud and put it on the blind man's eyes (see John 9:6). Could it be He used the mud not because of some deep theological reason, but just because Jesus likes to be childlike and play in the mud with His Father? When Jesus reached out with mud on His hands, He knew the Father was also reaching out and creating with Him.

> O Lord, for I hide myself in You! (Psalm 143:9)

> When He had said this, He spat on the ground and made mud with His saliva, and He spread the mud [like an ointment] on the man's eyes. (John 9:6)

> I and the Father are one. (John 10:30)

Tunnel under the Throne

During worship, I saw a tunnel that ran under the throne and the ballroom floor in Heaven. As we sang "Holy, Holy, Holy," our praise raised the floor and the throne of God was literally high and lifted up because of the praises of the people. Our praise reached Heaven (see Isaiah 6:1)! The floor and the throne were bright white and radiant. They were high and lifted up. It's like when a stage rises from the center at a concert.

> I saw the Lord sitting upon a throne, high and lifted up, and the skirts of His train filled the [most holy part of the] temple. (Isaiah 6:1)

Holy Spirit Has Light Hair

I was sitting on the front porch at home when I saw the Holy Spirit in the spirit realm. If someone in the natural had been sitting with me, they would not have seen Him. He appeared to me as having long, blond, wavy, hair with blue eyes, through which He can see the universe.

He said, "I will be on your left side always holding your hand. I feel more comfortable on the left side," and He laughed. I also saw an angel and I instantly knew his name was 'The Enforcer'. He was tall, muscular, and a very powerful looking angel!

> White hair is a crown of glory and is seen most among the godly. (Proverbs 16:31 TLB)

Holy Spirit Loves the ER

The Lord Jesus said to me, "You want to time travel!"

Then I saw white lights flashing by. And then I saw the Holy Spirit's blond hair and blue eyes, so I knew He was also there.

I had apparently time-traveled and Jesus said, "I would like to introduce you to someone." Kathryn Kuhlman stepped into view. (Instantly I was reminded that we are surrounded by so great a cloud of witnesses as described in Hebrews.)

She said, "Hi, Kim! I've wanted sooooo to meet you! You read my book and didn't criticize me! Now I get the chance to teach you about Holy Spirit."

Then I watched as she put Him on. She clothed herself with Him and walked with Him.

Clothed in Him, she said to me, "Oh come in!" I walked into the Holy Spirit and felt tingly all over. She said, "Oh, He loves the emergency room! Take Him with you when you volunteer in the emergency room."

(You can learn more about Kathryn Kuhlman at:
http:// kathrynkuhlman.com)

> Therefore then, since we are surrounded by so great a cloud of witnesses, let us strip off and throw aside every encumbrance (unnecessary weight) and that sin which so readily clings to and entangles us. And let us run with patient endurance and steady and active persistence that appointed course of the race that is set before us. (Hebrews 12:1)

You Heard Their Cries

I turned on some worship music and sat down on the floor of my prayer room. I began to quiet my mind and body from the day and just rest and soak in the presence of Jesus. I sat on the floor because that's what I like to do. A person can sit, lie down, or stand, whatever helps you to focus on Jesus. I keep paper beside me so if I am reminded of someone I need to call or think of a task I need to do, I write it down. That way my mind stays clear from distractions.

As I got quiet I felt the presence of Jesus, and felt a drawing as I stepped over into the spirit realm by faith. "Ascending" or "stepping over into the spirit" is a love tool to develop our relationship with Daddy God, Jesus our Bridegroom, and the Holy Spirit. I was suddenly sitting at a table, as an adult, with Daddy God, Jesus, and the Holy Spirit. Daddy began to unroll my scroll and read it out loud. Again, I was hearing about my scroll.

Daddy said, "When I formed you, I reached and placed stars in your eyes to shine. I put a piece of My heart in you so you would never feel unloved or second best. I gathered the warmth from the sun and placed into you the streams and waterfalls. I watched you play at my feet and dance with others. As you grew, you heard the cries from the people on the earth and you ran to the edge to look over."

"As you grew more, the cries from their hearts grew louder and you ran to see, and began to cry and ask Me, 'Why do they cry, Daddy? Why are they hurting and so sad?' That's when I knew what pulled on you. I let you go to the hurting hearts."

As we do what we have been placed on the earth to do, let us not forget Jesus is coming soon for a beautiful bride who has learned who they are as the Bride of Christ.

> Then the angel said to me, "These words are trustworthy and true: 'I am coming soon!' God, who tells his prophets what the future holds, has sent his angel to tell you this will happen soon. Blessed are those who believe it and all else written in the scroll." (Revelation 22:6–7 TLB)

Blue Flower Canopy

During worship I stepped over into Heaven. I was a child and saw Daddy God. He smiled and was so glad to see me. We held hands and walked to His garden. It was thick with flowers. The colors were so bright and rich, the leaves and the petals were thick. The fragrance was so thick you could almost feel it. The garden was full of life.

We walked around looking at the garden and I sat under a canopy of the prettiest blue flowers—that sing! Well, all of the flowers in Heaven sing, but I was really drawn to the multiple shades of blue flowers so I especially noticed their music.

Daddy said, "This is our new go-to spot, and He smiled. I knew He meant this will be our place to sit and talk to each other. Daddy loves to hear from His children face to face. He wants a relationship with us, not just our worship. He wants us to see how He sees, so we can love like He loves.

Daddy Whittles

After seeing flecks of blue sparkles and shiny crystal specks, I found myself, as a child, sitting in the blue-flowered canopy chair in Daddy's garden. I could see Daddy sitting in front of me. He has the sweetest smile, and eyes that sparkle. His hair is long, white, and beautiful. I have never been a big Santa Claus fan, but picture the happiest, nicest, kindest Santa Claus, and that is sort of how He appeared to me in our garden at this time.

He said, "Can you smell the flowers?" I could literally *feel* the fragrance thickly covering my arms and face like a spray tan would cover you.

I felt a flame of fire on my left side as if an angel of fire was standing beside me. I felt like I was supposed to pull it into me and say, "Burn out what isn't to be there."

Then I was watching Daddy God as He was whittling something. He said, "It's for you!" Daddy looked to His left as someone walked up. I saw a man with black, wild-looking hair, a husky body, and big hands walk up. Daddy smiled at Him, raised His eyebrows, and looked at me.

This man said, "Hi, I'm Ezekiel. They didn't believe me, either."

I asked, "So how did you keep going?"

He said, "You must have a close relationship with the Father. You have to know that you know! I will show up and encourage you. In the meantime, read my book." He laughed and said, "They didn't believe me either, but I have a book! Read my entire book and I will impart revelation to you." Then He turned and walked away.

I stayed in the blue-flowered chair and watched Daddy whittle. He was using a knife and whittling on a stick.

Ezekiel is one of those in the cloud of witnesses who have passed on and stepped into Heaven. They watch us and I believe they are cheering for us to not stop, but to keep running the race like it says in Hebrews 12:1.

> Therefore then, since we are surrounded by so great a cloud of witnesses, let us strip off and throw aside every encumbrance (unnecessary weight) and that sin which so readily clings to and entangles us. And let us run with patient endurance and steady and active persistence that appointed course of the race that is set before us.

Soft, Fuzzy Animals

While I was sitting in my blue-flowered chair watching Daddy whittle, two little people came and took me to the river. I appeared as an adult and I had a different view of the river this time. It was now flat, wide, and slow moving. Joy, my daughter, was there in the river [see "The Children" on page 34].

I jumped on her and dunked her, and we laughed. Then we sat, and talked, and breathed underwater—at the bottom of the river! Joy showed me colored stones of green, ruby, and other colors. I picked them up and put them in my stomach as if it were a place to carry them. I was feeling a little like a kangaroo. Later she and I sat on the edge of the river kicking our feet and splashing in the water, and we heard the water drops singing!

Then a white, soft, fuzzy animal-like creature flew up to me, wrapping, rubbing, and rolling over me to dry me off.

Joy laughed and said, "Oh, they always do that." They were as soft as a chinchilla but were longer, like a ferret. They were so happy and *incredibly* soft. One rolled around my stomach and back, under my arms as I lifted them up, and around my neck. We laughed at my new discovery of these furry little guys.

She said, "I want to show you something." We walked to a huge field filled with green glowing lights on the ground. They were similar to Christmas lights, but were alive and growing. We lay down and I made movements like I was making snow angels. I scooped some of the lights up and put them in my stomach to carry them. We ran together and laughed so much. Soon some shiny lights began to rain down over me, and Joy said, "Just let the earth's problems go!"

Then I was back in the garden and sat with Daddy. He held my hands and said, "I like your worship, but I want your love!"

Ezekiel showed up again and said, "I went for a year without saying a word—and that's kind of where you are now. In the between times I developed my relationship with Him. Oh, still everyone watched everything I did, wondering if 'that' meant something spiritual or not." And he laughed.

Daddy said, "I like coming here (we were in His blue-flower garden) because I can just be Me to you. Your home is like your garden, where you don't have to be a secretary or spiritual leader, but can just be you to your family and close friends."

I've Got You

Daddy and I (as a child) went for a walk from the blue flower garden through a green archway into the open field alongside the river, and we sat with our legs dangling in the water.

He turned and said, "Here, taste this." It was a red berry milkshake type drink, and it was so good that I cried. I don't know why I cried. The shake was just so amazing and overwhelmingly good. He said, "The things I give you are good!"

We sat and drank by the water. I had no idea Daddy God liked milkshakes, but I sure was glad when He handed me one! I sipped it out of a straw and noticed that Daddy God didn't use a straw—but wow, the multi-flavors were incredible! God's milkshakes make your mouth come alive with tingling sensations.

Then I noticed that gardenias began to grow around me. I had forgotten about how much I love these plants.

He wrapped His arms around me as we sat by the river and He kept saying to me, "I've got you! I've got you, baby, I've got you!" He wants us to know we are safe in His arms.

Some people are so performance driven, when what God really wants is a relationship of just sitting and talking back and forth with us.

Daddy's So Nice

I sat next to Daddy in our blue flower garden and He was grieving that His children thought He would hurt them.

He said, "I give you My heart for them." I felt bright, open joy and it began to rain brightly colored flower petals, they were falling everywhere. I told Daddy that I would go to the hurting hearts to heal them from the lies the devil had told them. Daddy God is so nice and He would never hurt His child.

> See what kind of love the Father has given to us in that we should be called God's children, and that is what we are! Because the world didn't recognize him, it doesn't recognize us. (John 3:1 CEB)

2014

Daddy God's Hair

I turned on some soothing worship music, quieted my mind from the day, focused my thoughts on Jesus, and after just a few minutes I was over in the spirit realm. Once again I saw the garden with my chair made of real, live, blue flowers (which were firm enough to sit on), and Daddy God was waiting for me.

Appearing as a child, I ran up to Him, hugged Him, and asked, "Have you had a hug today?" He laughed and placed His big Daddy arms around me as I put my face on His chest with my arms around Him. Not in any hurry, we just hugged each other and enjoyed the love between us.

I asked Him, "May I brush your hair?"

He said, "I would love to have My hair brushed!" Why I asked this question seemed odd to me, but I guess He gave me the desire.

While brushing His hair, I noticed each hair strand was thick and alive. Each one looked like a tube that I could see into, to a different location. I could see a waterfall in one strand, and ocean waves in another. Each strand of His hair made a different sound. One made the sound of a light breeze, one made the sound of ocean waves, another sounded like waterfalls, yet another was the sound of flowers singing worship, and some strands sounded like the wind blowing through the trees. I put my face in His hair and just listened and absorbed the gentle sounds. It was so amazing and breathtaking. I didn't ever want to do anything else but stay with my face buried in Daddy's hair, listening and smelling His fragrance.

After what seemed like a short time, He smiled and was pleased with my new discovery. He put His big strong Daddy hands under my arms and lifted me up to His back and gave me a piggy-back ride. We walked to the edge of a cliff and looked down over the greenest valley.

He said, "This is one of My favorite spots." Then with His big strong hands, He lifted me higher onto His shoulders so I could see better. But all I wanted at this time was to bury my face into His hair so I slid down His back and pulled His hair over to cover me.

He smiled and said, "I created Samson with a desire to have His hair messed with too. That was a part of "My enjoyment" that I incorporated in a human form."

We walked back to our blue flower garden and sat down. I put both of my hands on His face so I could look at His face, eyes, and eyebrows.

Then said, "Wow, what if I really am doing this? Oh my God—it's God!"

He laughed heartily and said, "Don't analyze it, just go with it." I sat and pulled His hair over His shoulders and put it on my head so it was dangling down my face like a long wig. He laughed at my child-likeness!

As Daddy had been whittling something out of wood for me, I asked Him, "How is my woodcarving going?"

Daddy said, "I'm still working on it."

I said, "Take your time. No, wait, take *my* time. If you take Your time I'll be really old!"

He just laughed and said, "I do love your expressions!"

Daddy God Turned Transparent!

After turning on some worship music, getting my mind quiet, and praying in tongues, I stepped over by faith into the spirit realm. I saw Daddy God, I ran up to Him as a child, and gave Him a big hug. He was extremely happy for me to come see Him. We held hands and walked along a beach.

As I held His big strong hand, I asked Him, "What do you like about the beach?"

He said, "I like the way the sun reflects on the water, like sparkling diamonds. I like the little crabs that poke their heads out to say 'hi' and then run and duck in the sand." He laughed.

He asked me what I liked, and I said, "Those too, and I like how my foot presses out the water and leaves a print, and I like those little birds that run really fast." He laughed and said, "I'm glad!"

While we were walking, talking, and holding hands, He turned transparent and said, "Go with me!" I walked into Him and we were instantly back at our garden park with the blue flowers. He said, "That's how we travel so easily. You're in Me, and where I go, you go!"

I stood up, walked over, sat next to Him, and again began to brush His hair. I couldn't help myself and just had to bury my face in it once more. I heard Him laugh. His hair is so incredibly amazing!

See, Follow, Hear, Follow with Your Heart

After listening to a few minutes of peaceful worship music, by faith I stepped over into the spirit realm. Knowing that either Jesus or Daddy God would be there to meet me, I saw Daddy God and we hugged (I was a child). He was so happy to see me! He loves when His children come to be with Him.

We held hands and began to walk. We went out into a large field that was wide open. The green grass was rich in color and the clean fresh air was full of life. Suddenly multi-colored flower petals that sang, began to fall around us. We continued to walk, holding hands in the singing, falling flower petals.

I unexpectedly had an overwhelming knowing on the inside of me. It was this revelation: "Out of His love for me, He gave me everything. Everything was made for me and given to me because He loves me so much."

Then I knew that out of His love for me He gave me the Holy Spirit! I received the gift of the Holy Spirit because this was a gift of love from God, for me!

Doubt would make me think that I couldn't see or hear the Holy Spirit, but that's a lie. Why would Daddy give me a gift I couldn't see? The truth is that having a relationship with the Holy Spirit comes with the gift of love Daddy gave me.

Then I heard Daddy say, "Your eyes will burn with fire as never before. Your natural eyes won't see what the eyes of your heart see. See with the eyes of your heart (Ezekiel 3:10). Follow the eyes of your heart. Hear with the ears of your heart. Follow the ears of your heart."

> Moreover he said unto me, Son of man, all my words that I shall speak unto thee receive in thy heart, and hear with thine ears. (Ezekiel 3:10 ASV)

Enlarge My Spirit

I was taking a bath one night when I felt the presence of Daddy God in the room. I closed my eyes and by faith I stepped into Heaven, and I showed up in our blue flower garden, this time as an adult.

Daddy said, "Come with me. I want to show you something." He began to walk hunched over with a cane. He looked at me and said, "This is how you think I am: old, like an old man. But this is how I really am!" Then He stood up straight and tall—and to me He looked big, like twelve feet tall, and He was strong!

He said, "But I am never too big to hold your hand!"

He opened a hope chest full of bright, shiny, gold treasures that looked like balls. He said, "Scoop them up and put them in you!" So, over and over again I scooped up these shiny, sparkly, gold treasures and put them in my spirit.

Then I began to say, "Enlarge my spirit to hold God's treasures—the things God thinks are valuable. Enlarge my spirit!" I felt my stomach get fuller and fuller.

He said, "This is what you will pray over people in the prayer line: 'Enlarge your spirit to hold the treasures of God!'"

The world didn't receive when Jesus was trying to reveal the Father's nature and His love for them, but He didn't stop telling of His Father. Jesus said,

> Righteous Father, though the world does not know you, I know you, and they know that you have sent me. I have made you known to them, and will continue to make you known in order that the love you have for me may be in them and that I myself may be in them." (John 17:25 NIV)

Chapter 3

Animals and Angels in Heaven

2009–2011

Butterflies

During worship, I stepped over in the spirit realm and I was an adult. I saw brightly colored red, orange, and yellow butterflies that changed color as they flew. I also saw water that sparkled, and songs of praises rose from the sparkles.

Jesus said, "When you are here, you won't remember the days you spent 'there' (pointing to the earth). Those days are earthen days, not forever days. Let them go!"

> Don't worry about anything; instead, pray about everything; tell God your needs, and don't forget to thank him for his answers. (Philippians 4:6 TLB)

Pets in Heaven

I had been spending time worshiping, when I stepped into Heaven and saw Jesus standing there smiling. He came up to me (I was an adult) and gave me two big hugs, not those side hugs, but big hugs!

While I was standing there talking to Jesus, I saw a medium-sized, long-haired, light brown dog that jumped up on me with her front paws and looked sweetly up at me. I reached down to pet her on the head, thinking, "What a sweet and pretty dog!" I remembered that my husband and I were just talking about what kind of dog we should get, but we couldn't decide.

Jesus looked at me, and smiled like He knew something I didn't know. Then Jesus and I, with this cocker spaniel following us, went for a walk.

And then, this same cocker spaniel, a light brown haired dog showed up on my family's front porch three days later! We named her Mia, and she is the perfect dog for us. But even though Mia was perfect and sent from Heaven, she was not house broken.

When I wondered about that, Jesus said, "In Heaven you don't have to go to the bathroom because that would be waste. And you don't recycle. This is your Father you are dealing with, and he knows better than you what you need." (Matthew 6:8 MSG)

I'm in the Army of the Lord

I was trying to pray one night and going through all the "stuff" of repenting, pleading the blood, and so on, and Jesus said, "Stop all that stuff and come here." He hugged me and swirled me around and put both of us on a white horse (I was an adult), and we began to ride fast. He said, "Put your head down," and we rode really fast up over hills and down through a field. There were other riders on white horses that we were following.

He said, "Take the reins," and He seemed to scoot off. I slid up front without Him. I rode by myself and then noticed that Jesus was following along beside me, without a horse! I could see a line of other riders, in front and behind, on white horses (see Revelation 19).

Jesus said, "They are also learning to ride. You are in the Army of the Lord. And this Army is going to battle. Your enemy is the spirit of perversion that comes against children causing them to be molested! You will win because you have the Lord God behind you as your backup. You can't lose this battle. Each time you come to pray, be prepared to ride. Your horse's name is Peal, like peals of thunder—rippling thunder or power."

Jesus put on me a breastplate of armor, including a covering for my head, arms, legs, and feet. He said, "You are in the Army of the Lord. Be prepared to ride!"

Later in prayer, I felt rose petals by the thousands falling all around me. As they swirled in circles, I could smell the flower petals and hear music coming from them; it filled the air.

Then I saw and felt my white horse. He was as soft as a chinchilla, with hair as thick as a lion's. He (the horse) said, "I won't hurt you. I won't lie down and crush you. I won't rub against a tree and hurt your leg." He bent his head down low so I could jump on his bare back. We walked slowly and rode to a stream.

He bent down to get a drink. I was worried he would throw me over his head, but he said, "I won't bend and throw you over my head, I won't hurt you." In Heaven, the animals' mouths don't seem to move, but you can hear everything they are saying clearly. I usually spoke to Peal with my spoken words even though he heard my thoughts.

I got off and touched the water that he was drinking from. It was thick, shined like oil, and sparkled. He said, "It comes from the throne."

Peal lifted his head and said, "More riders are arriving."

One tall guy stopped and got off his horse beside us and said, "I will be with you, I will ride beside you all the way. When you're afraid, look and you will see me beside you. I will be with you always!" Instantly I understood that he was an angel assigned to me.

Peal and I rode really fast and after a while stopped. I got off and lay in the tall thick green grass to rest. Peal lay beside me. Again I worried that He would kick me with his big hoofs and he said, "I won't lie and kick you; I won't hurt you. Trust me, master."

Later when he (Peal) left, he first trotted off but then like a jet, he took off! The angel with me laughed and said, "You thought you rode fast!"

> After that I saw Heaven opened and behold a white horse [appeared] … and the troops of Heaven clothed in fine linen, dazzling and clean, followed Him on white horses. … Then I saw the beast and the rulers and leaders of the earth with their troops mustered to go into battle and make war against Him Who is mounted on the horse and against His troops. (Revelation 19:11, 14, 19)

Riding in Darkness

Peal (my horse in Heaven) came up to me (I was an adult). I petted him and got on his back, then we rode into a tall grassy field. And suddenly he jumped over an edge and we went down over a cliff and kept going down and down and down! I was a little scared, but I knew I would be safe. I looked to my right and the angel that I was introduced to earlier was there riding down beside me on his horse.

Then I realized we were extremely high above the earth, and Peal said, "Put your arms out and let go. I won't hurt you!" I did and we rode into darkness that was like a tunnel. As we went through the darkness, it retracted from us, like magnets turned backward.

Then I heard Jesus say, "You are in Me and I am in you. Darkness can't stay where there is life. Wave your arms" (1 John 1:5). As I did, the darkness repelled. My arms were like a flashlight. While moving my arms, the darkness backed off. The Lord said, "Don't be afraid of the darkness. It cannot stay around you!" It was so fun to ride that fast going through darkness and having it move back from you as you approached it and not being afraid of the dark.

And this is the message [the message of promise] which we have heard from Him and now are reporting to you: God is Light, and there is no darkness in Him at all [no, not in any way]. (1 John 1:5)

Riding a Huge Eagle

I was worshiping Jesus, and felt such peace come over me as I lay on the floor of my prayer room soaking in His presence. I stepped into the spirit realm and saw Jesus.

He said, "This isn't the end, but the beginning. Live your life for eternity." Instantly I was riding on a huge white eagle (see Exodus 19:4) the size of an airplane, and its wings were folding up and down. I heard, "You are riding into eternity."

"You saw what I did to the Egyptians, and how I lifted you up on eagle's wings and brought you to me." (Exodus 19:4 CEB)

Talk to the Animals

In Heaven you can talk to the animals (see Numbers 22:28-29). Their mouths don't seem to move, but you know what they are thinking and saying to you. I spoke out loud to them, but you don't have to. The conversation is so clear and easy to understand. And yes, you do feel a little like Dr. Doolittle!

Later, I was worshiping Jesus when instantly I was in Heaven, lying in the soft thick green grass as an adult. In Heaven the grass is very thick and soft; each blade is full of life, and the color is so deep with no sign at all of death.

My horse Peal came up and nuzzled me. I knew he wanted me to get on and ride. I got on and we rode fast, just letting the air blow past us. When I say fast, it's like jet speed but gentle at the same time. After riding for a while we stopped, and I saw Jesus.

When you think you want to do something, instantly you are where you want to be. When I saw Jesus, I wanted to be beside Him, so instantly I was. He was holding a fresh, clean robe and reached out and put it on me.

He also had fresh oil in a pitcher and began to pour it over me. It felt so refreshing and peaceful.

Jesus poured perfume on me and said, "You smell good. Remember, things like this will come." (He was referring to the heaviness on my heart). "When they do, come to Me and spend time with Me. Cross over from the world into My presence. I will take care of the ones you love, but it is their choice to love Me. Love isn't love if I have to make them love Me!" I felt so peaceful and loved.

> And the Lord opened the mouth of the ass, and she said unto Balaam, What have I done unto thee, that thou hast smitten me these three times? And Balaam said unto the ass, Because thou hast mocked me: I would there were a sword in mine hand, for now would I kill thee. (Numbers 22:28-29 KJV)

Angel Named 'Entertaining'

While sitting on an airplane on my way to Redding, California, I was looking outside from my window seat. I was surprised to see someone on the wing of the plane, goofing off! I looked around the plane knowing a child must be watching a Harpo/Marx Brothers old comedy show, and this was a reflection on my window of some iPad.

However, there were no children on this flight. I looked behind me and in the other rows in front of me, but there was nothing playing! I looked back out my window and this "person" (who looked just like Harpo with fuzzy hair) waved at me! I thought, "Well, that's a coincidence." Since I was bored, I waved back at him and just leaned back, relaxed, and watched him. (see Hebrews 1:14)

I heard in my spirit, "He likes to show off!" He would act like he was in a canoe and would be paddling along with the wind of the airplane, and then he would get blown off. He would be walking against the wind like he was in a bad storm, with his head down while trudging along, and then he'd get blown off. He would do flips and rolls off the wing, and then act like he was crawling back up on the side of the wing. When we flew over a lake he acted like he was diving in a pool, and dove off the wing. He sat in a large chair, acting like he was reading a book, except the pages were blowing wildly because he was on the wing of a plane. The wind blew his book out of his hands so he jumped up to get it and flew off the wing. He would just show up and wave at me, and then let the wind blow him off.

He was very entertaining and funny. At one time I laughed out loud, then caught myself and looked around to see if anyone was watching me! This angel made me realize that what we think is fast, to the spirit world, it's really slow, or even has no effect. Suddenly Jesus appeared right next to my window looking at me—on the *outside* of the plane!

He said, while we watched this angel, "You think angels should be all military and stand at attention." While Jesus was saying this, the angel got up and stood at attention with a salute, then he got blown off the wing.

Jesus smiled and continued saying, "But they all do different things." I realized this angel could hear what Jesus was saying to me while I was inside the plane, and Jesus was outside the plane, all while we were traveling at 300 miles per hour.

Jesus said, "Angels are sent as ministering spirits. You were bored, so 'Entertaining' was sent to entertain you!"

While I was watching out the window of the plane, I had the realization that it was going so drastically slower than when I fly with Jesus in Heaven. When Jesus and I fly, the ground is a blur.

Jesus also said, "See how long it would take to get you to someone who was ready to commit suicide? I can send you there instantly like I did with Paul. My people could minister all over the world. Would you do that?"

I said, "Yes!"

Later I was working out at the local gym on one of the weight machines. Sometimes when I work out, I close my eyes so I can concentrate and keep track of how many repetitions I've done. Each time I closed my eyes, at this particular time, I saw this angel named 'Entertaining' (the same one I saw on the wing of the airplane who entertained me). The angel was acting like he was lifting heavy weights and would make faces like he was straining, but there would be nothing in his hands. At one point he was curling a real cat but again was acting like he was really straining. It was very funny and entertaining! Note that at the gym I could only see him with my eyes closed; that is called a closed vision.

> Are not the angels all ministering spirits (servants) sent out in the service [of God for the assistance] of those who are to inherit salvation? (Hebrews 1:14)

Riding a Horse in Heaven

Pam Finlay ©2014

During worship, if you will trust what you see and not doubt, Jesus will show you amazing fun things. I was worshiping at church and after a few minutes of basking in His presence, I got quiet and was not thinking about the words we were singing. I was instantly on my horse in Heaven as an adult, riding really fast. I let go of the reins and stretched out my arms. I felt so free and full of life again, letting all the cares of the world blow off!

Later during worship, I felt an angel blow on the side of my face and then after a while I felt blowing on the front of my face. It felt as if someone had a fan pointing at me, like a gust of wind. I opened my eyes to make sure someone wasn't blowing on me. No one was standing close to me, fanning me or blowing on my face, so I knew it was the angel letting me know he was close by. I am learning that when I feel his presence, a healing is going to take place during the prayer time which is offered toward the end of our worship service.

2012–2014

Fighting on a Horse

While praying in the spirit (in tongues) and quieting down my mind and body, I crossed over into the spirit realm—as an adult. Peal, my horse, instantly came up to me. I got on and we rode. His hair is extremely soft and long. He galloped even though we were riding on air. I saw that other riders were with me. Then I saw Jesus way up front as He turned to look and smile at me, making sure I was okay.

We all stopped around a hole and circled like Indians. We were looking down through this hole, or portal, when Jesus said, "The enemy is planning an attack to uproot and scatter any seeds that have been planted, but have not yet rooted. There are those whose hearts are hardened like the Pharisees. They won't listen and will be angry and leave because they 'know' they are right. There are those who are weak and will blow away easily. Then there are those who want to know if what they have been told is true. Those are the ones we're fighting for. Hold up your shields! Hold up your shields!" We rode down through the portal to fight!

Other seed [of the same kind] fell among thorn plants, and the thistles grew and pressed together and utterly choked and suffocated it, and it yielded no grain. And other seed [of the same kind] fell into good (well-adapted) soil and brought forth grain, growing up and increasing, and yielded up to thirty times as much, and sixty times as much, and even a hundred times as much as had been sown. (Mark 4:7–8)

Riding a Lion in the Blood

I went into my prayer room, turned on soft worship music and began to worship Jesus. Almost instantly, with my eyes closed, I saw a hairy angel in the spirit realm. He grabbed me and said, "Come. You need to go." Immediately I was an adult riding on the back of a large hairy lion.

I had a sword and pointed it forward and yelled, "Charge!" We flew through cancerous brown cells. I yelled "Life! Life!" and white light cells burst forth. In the spirit, you find yourself doing things you never thought of doing and may not even know why you are doing them until it's over.

Riding on the back of this huge lion, we rode, yelling and declaring "Life," and watched white light cells form. I knew we were in a bloodstream and inside of a brain.

Then Daddy said, "Don't let the devil win! In Me is life. When you were in the river, do you remember the life? In the waterfall is life, remember? In the plants is life. Jesus came to give life and life more abundantly! Speak life to every sickness, disease, disorder—life! Don't let the devil win. Jesus has paid the price for life! Speak life to the blood, speak life! Don't let the devil win!"

> The thief cometh not, but for to steal, and to kill, and to destroy: I am come that they might have life, and that they might have it more abundantly. (John 10:10 KJV)

Angel and His Robe

I went into my prayer room and turned on some instrumental worship music and began to worship Jesus. Within a few minutes of tuning into Jesus, and turning my mind off of the everyday events, I stepped over into the spirit realm and found myself, as a child, sitting on Daddy God's lap. He is so happy when His kids come into His presence and come up to Him boldly without fear.

While sitting on His lap, I saw a beautiful angel with a beard, holding a staff and wearing a hooded, robed gown with gold trim. His gown was big and full and beautiful. I slid off of Daddy's lap to see this angel.

I said to the angel as I touched and rubbed His robe, "This is so pretty!" He leaned forward down to me and said, "It's pretty comfortable, too," and then threw His head back and laughed! Daddy God and everyone laughed; this angel was so big and pretty!

They never laugh at you mocking or making fun of you in Heaven, but they do laugh at some of the funny things we say or do.

Angel Named Tom

While sleeping, I saw a bright flash in my room. I woke up and asked, "What was that light, Jesus?"

He said, "One of your angels."

I asked, "What's his name and what does he do?" He said, "His name is Tom and he protects you!" From this time on, I have been able to sense his presence, standing guard at my window.

> For He will give His angels [especial] charge over you to accompany and defend and preserve you in all your ways [of obedience and service]. (Psalm 91:11)

Flying on an Eagle

After spending time worshiping Jesus in my prayer room, I was instantly flying high above the trees, as an adult, on the back of a gigantic eagle. We were flying as high as planes fly.

I heard, "You will be flying high above the rest." I could feel his feathers under my hands and see the great length of his huge wings. I could feel the strength as he lifted and lowered his wings so gracefully, but with power. I could feel the wind blowing against my face as I looked over his wings down to the towns below. I felt strengthened and refreshed as I rode high above the earth, above the noise and chaos.

> But those who wait for the Lord shall change and renew their strength and power; they shall lift their wings and mount up [close to God] as eagles [mount up to the sun]; they shall run and not be weary, they shall walk and not faint or become tired. (Isaiah 40:31)

Angels Replaced What Was Missing

I was playing with my old camcorder and rereading the directions because it had been a long time since I'd used it. One disc was in the recorder, but there were three disc covers (which are clear and see-through), they were empty. I opened all three covers, as if I couldn't see they were empty, and wondered where the discs had gone to! I'm always diligent to put them back in their covers for protection.

The following day I went back to read the directions to the camcorder again, and noticed that all three discs were there — one was in the camera, and the other two were in their disc cases! These cases were empty the day before, and now they had their discs in them—and I didn't do it! Angels? I think so. I had just been listening to Bill Johnson that day about a message on angels bringing things back that were lost!

> For He will give His angels [especial] charge over you to accompany and defend and preserve you in all your ways [of obedience and service]. (Psalm 91:11)

Dancing Fairy

I saw the prettiest dancing fairy angel with long, huge, multicolored feathers. She danced on feather-like feet. With her colorful wings she would push a powdery substance up and over to me. While she was praising Jesus, I saw that her face and legs were dainty and beautiful, her wings, or feathers, were very very long, and changed colors; they were also very large but light in weight, almost like a hummingbird.

> You're the one, God, you alone; You made the Heavens, the Heavens of Heavens, and all angels; The earth and everything on it, the seas and everything in them; You keep them all alive; Heaven's angels worship you! (Nehemiah 9:5–6 MSG)

Mermaid-Type Water Angel

I saw this long, tall, water-angel being. She was on top of a water-like substance. Her body and arms seemed like a half-mile long and her hair seemed endless. As she worshiped, she swirled her hair across the sky. Her endless-looking hair painted the universe with bright beautiful colors. With each swipe, each hair strand painted a different color. She was so beautiful, I still feel an "awe" as I remember seeing her. I didn't hear words or music coming from her, but somehow, worship was filling the universe while she worshiped the Lord of Lords!

Bridegroom's Chamber and Angel Erin

Jesus took me into His chamber. It was an intimate room with furniture such as a handmade wooden chest of drawers and dressers that you typically might find in a bedroom. But what really drew my attention was a soft, fluffy cloud-like substance on the wall! I couldn't help but scoop it off and put it in me. I put it in my eyes, ears, stomach, heart, and so forth (Song of Solomon 1:4).

Jesus said, "It's intimacy that you're putting in you—intimacy of and for Me. And I am giving you an angel dressed in purple to see you along your journey back to the Bridegroom's Chamber, just like in the Bible. He will tell you of Me along the way and escort you home, to My home." His name is Erin, which means Peace.

I got the impression that when I come back to Heaven from the earth, possibly for good, Erin would lead me back to this room where just Jesus and I can be alone together. And don't worry, everyone will have Jesus all to themselves; but of course, not in any sexual type way. This time spent in the Chamber will be for Jesus and you to be quiet and focus on each other. It will be like a princess might have a personal assistant to take care of her. Jesus wants to take care of our every need.

A few days after this encounter in the Chamber, I went (in the natural) to a county fair with rides, food, and games. I stood staring at the cotton candy machine. The man took a hollow tube and gently rolled this tube lightly around in the soft-spun, sweet cotton candy. He did not force it along the edges, but gently rolled the tube, allowing the soft sweet cotton-like substance to attach itself to the tube. When he pulled it out, the hollow tube was now covered in this sweet cotton candy substance that just melts in your mouth.

This is exactly the way I felt in the Chamber when I was putting the puffy clouds all over my body. I felt like I was being covered and rolled in soft, cottony sweet goodness.

As I walked outside and looked up, the sky wasn't typically cloudy, but was covered in those small fluffy little clouds that I saw on Jesus' Chamber walls. I was overwhelmed that Jesus had been displaying in the sky His feeling of intimacy toward us all along. If I'd never had an encounter in

Jesus' Chamber, I would not have seen the puffy clouds in the sky as Jesus' desire for intimacy with His bride.

> Draw me! We will run after you! The king brings me into his (chamber) apartments! We will be glad and rejoice in you! We will recall [when we were favored with] your love, more fragrant than wine. The upright [are not offended at your choice, but sincerely] love you. (Song of Solomon 1:4)

Butterfly Angels Worship

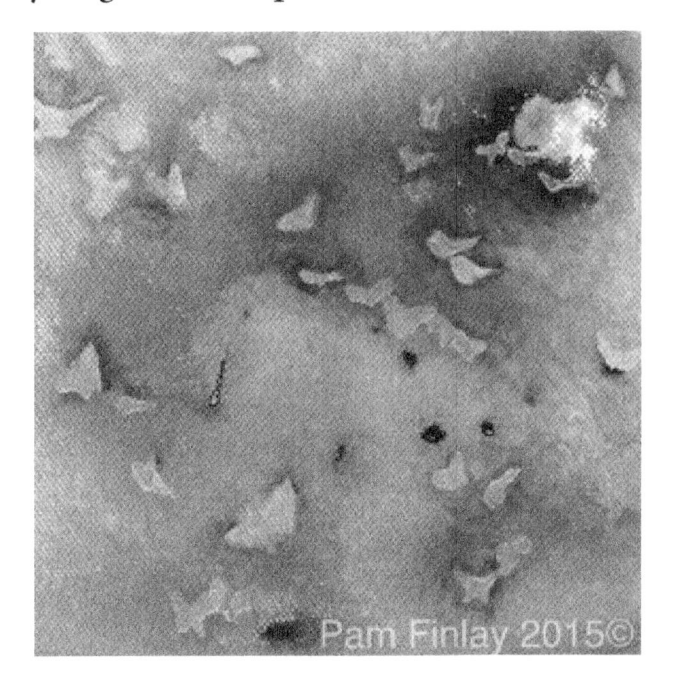

During worship, my spiritual eyes were opened and I saw different-sized angels. Some were big and some were very small, but these all looked like butterflies. When they moved in any direction, music and notes came through their wings. Their wings were thin with tiny holes that seemed to make music as they moved, as if the holes were filtering the air and turning it into music. There were a bunch of angels flying around me and each one made different music. I held my hands out and many small ones fluttered and sat covering my hands and fingers. Even when they were slowly moving their wings, worship music still filtered through their wings. It was amazing!

God said, "When His children lift their hands during worship, angels will sit on their hands and worship with us, and fill the room with music."

Psalm 134:2 NIV says, "Lift up your hands in the sanctuary and praise the Lord."

Angel Called Prosperity

During worship Daddy God said, "I have a surprise for you!" He brought me to the biggest, most beautiful, rainbow-colored, butterfly-shaped angel I'd ever seen.

Daddy said, "The angel's name is Prosperity, and she will be assigned to you forever!" I asked the angel to bring "inspiration, ideas, and buyers." I teared up because of her beauty and her colors that kept changing.

She smiled and said "I am made by your Father."

Things in Heaven are so overwhelming and beautiful. Later that night, my husband and I both saw a white flash of light in the room next to us! We looked at each other and asked if the other one saw it. I had a sense that the angel had made an appearance.

Fun House

I felt a tall angel on my right side and he said, "I'm taking you to the Fun House." I saw two large squares the size of doors: one white and one red. They looked like square cards (I was a teenager).

I felt impressed to flip one over, so I flipped over the white one and the angel said, "Go in." I stepped in, and saw we were at the top of a huge slide.

I jumped on and slid around and down, up over hills and down huge drops. I was laughing all the way. Then I was instantly back at the beginning.

I felt that now I was to flip over the other square card-door. I flipped the red one and saw nothing. The angel said, "Go in!" By faith I stepped into nothing and later learned this was called the "No Gravity Room." I floated around with no gravity, laughing as I watched others in the room having fun with me. Heaven is fun!

Chapter 4

People and other Fun Events

I am reminded of Paul's vision:

> I know a man in Christ who fourteen years ago— whether in the body I do not know, or out of the body I do not know, [only] God knows—such a man was caught up to the third Heaven. And I know that such a man—whether in the body or out of the body I do not know, [only] God knows. (2 Corinthians 12:2-3)

1995–2000

Meeting Daniel, Joshua, Moses, Noah, Ruth, and David

I heard Jesus say, "I'm going to take you and show you something you have never seen." I felt quietness come over me as an angel ushered me into a room. I was an adult. I saw Jesus, and He came up to me and gave me a kiss like He always does.

Then the angel said, "I'm going to take you to meet some of the head men." I saw a long table with four men sitting around one end; they were all talking together. The angel introduced me to them by saying "This is Kim." They looked up and smiled.

The angel said, "This is Daniel, this is Joshua, this is Moses, and this is Noah" while pointing to each one. The angel pulled my chair out so I could sit down. I was feeling embarrassed at not knowing why I was there.

He said, "You can ask them whatever you want."

With the lion's den in mind I asked Daniel, "How did you know it was God? How did you know that God would do something for you?" Daniel had wide shoulders and a moustache. His hair was light to medium brown and looked as if it was pulled back in a ponytail. He sat up tall and straight, keeping his hands folded on the dark brown, shiny table top.

Daniel said, "I know God by His love. I knew God would do whatever had to be done to ensure I wasn't hurt."

I turned to Joshua, who was strongly built with muscular arms and hands, and very wide shoulders. He seemed to be very tall, maybe six to seven feet and his hair was short and wavy. He had a moustache and short beard. I could feel a sense of strength and knowledge about him.

With the wall of Jericho in mind I asked him, "How did you know it was God?"

Joshua said, "I know God as my deliverer and strength. I knew that whatever enemy I was facing, it was an enemy of God's. The people of Jericho did evil in God's sight, so I knew God would help us conquer them, in His name. I knew He would do whatever had to be done to accomplish that: Whether He was going to tell me their plans, or show me how to go around from a different angle, or whether He would do it supernaturally. I knew God would destroy the enemy that I was facing—not the enemy way behind me or the enemy way off over there, or over there (waving his hands

People and other Fun Events

---

left and right), but the enemy I was facing at that time. I knew God would bring down my enemy, because they were also His enemy." He spoke with such confidence and strength about knowing the walls would actually come down.

I turned to Moses, who had long, white hair and a black medium-length beard (not a real long one like he is portrayed on TV). He seemed older than Daniel and Joshua.

With the Red Sea in mind I asked him the same question. Moses said, "I know God as my Provision. If He had to be a cloud to protect us from the scorching sun, if He had to be water so we could drink, if He had to be the manna so we could eat, I knew He would be those things. At first, when I stretched my rod over the water, I thought God would harden it, and we would walk on it. I was just as surprised as everyone else when it split." He leaned forward and laughed.

He continued, "I knew as we stood there that God would do something to protect us from the enemy who was coming upon us to destroy God's people. I didn't know what it would be because the sea was so big and deep, but I knew God would do something." Moses talked using his hands a lot.

I turned to Noah who had long, white hair—and I couldn't see his face well because I was being disturbed by the people making noise in the room (back on earth) . I had to really stay focused on what he was saying.

But with the ark in mind I asked Noah, "At the beginning when you first decided to start building this big project, how did you know it was God telling you to build it?"

He said, "I know God as my Protector from disaster and destruction. When my kids were young, there were men who would plan attacks against the boys, and God would warn me in advance. They would plan to burn our houses down and kill our children, animals, and pets but God would warn us in advance."

Noah was deep in thought, and then said, "God always provided protection because any of those attacks would have been disastrous to our family." He had a deep love and concern for his family.

He continued, "When God told me to build an ark, the big boat, and gave me the plans, I knew He was once again making a way for my family to escape a disaster." Noah's face changed and he said with concern, "You know, God so much wanted for everyone to be able to come. He was so concerned about them. I tried to tell the people—I tried—but they wouldn't listen to me. They only mocked and laughed at me. I knew God was preparing to protect us from a disaster."

Noah seemed to be a thinker and a guy who tried to figure things out. He didn't feel sadness at this time, but knew God's heart was for the people.

These men I talked to all knew God in a very absolute, unshakable way. They knew God! Daniel knew God by His love. Joshua knew God by His deliverance and strength. Moses knew God by His provision. And Noah knew God by His protection.

Jesus then introduced me to Ruth, Abraham, Benjamin, David, and many others who I don't recall (see Hebrew 12:1).

Later, Jesus took me to another meeting room. I saw my grandma sitting by my stepdad. And then pointing to a room full of people, Jesus said, "These are relatives."

In front of everyone, Jesus scooped His hands together and poured oil over my hands and said, "I, with the power of the Holy Spirit (who I could see standing by Jesus), anoint you with a healing anointing that no man can give."

> Therefore, since we are surrounded by such a great cloud of witnesses, let us throw off everything that hinders and the sin that so easily entangles. And let us run with perseverance the race marked out for us. (Hebrews 12:1 NIV)

Translated to Arabia, Turkey, and China

I had been worshiping Jesus when He took my hand and we went to Arabia (I was an adult). Instantly, we were in a worship service. A lady came dancing by, worshiping Jesus, while the others worshiped too, not caring that a woman was dancing before Jesus. Jesus loves it! And the people in the meeting didn't care because it was common for women to dance and worship Jesus. No one watched her with a critical eye (like some religious groups might do). Jesus was showing me that it's okay with Him if someone dances during worship.

Jesus took my hand and we were instantly in Turkey where believers were worshiping with communion. Each took a bite of bread and drank out of a goblet and then passed the items to the next person.

They said, "We are partaking of Jesus' body and blood."

Then we went to China where believers bowed in worship. And then we went to Africa where believers used bright colored materials to wave in worship to Jesus.

Jesus said, "America worships as David worshipped in dance and singing. They have some communion, some waving of flags or materials, and some bowing. There are many different ways to worship Me."

At this time in my life, there was a lot of controversy over waving flags during worship, dancing, and whether we should take communion this way or that, but now I see that they are *all* enjoyed by Jesus.

Popping Bones

Again I walked, as an adult, through the Hall of Elements. I looked through the glass wall into a room which was filled with bones bouncing and vibrating with life, ready to be received by people who needed new bones on earth.

The Lord said, "Bones without life shrivel up. And when the marrow is gone, they become crooked, thin, and twisted. But with life they pop straight (Proverbs 3:7–8). Many will come to you for prayer, so speak life to their bones." I could hear what sounded like popcorn popping.

> Do not be wise in your own eyes; fear the Lord and shun evil. This will bring health to your body and nourishment to your bones. (Proverbs 3:7–8 NIV)

The Changing Room

During worship I was taken up into Heaven and began to walk around, as an adult, and found myself talking to Jesus. I was greeted by Ruth (from the Bible) who was standing nearby with some other people. Then I knew there was what Heaven calls a "Changing Room" in front of me, and I wanted to see what it was.

I am a really short brunette and have spent hours in tanning beds, wanting to be darker, so I thought, "I'd love to be a tall black lady!" And with that in mind, I walked into this room and was almost instantly changed into a tall black lady with beautiful, long and thick black hair!

Somehow I knew that this wouldn't last long so I thought, "I'm going to walk around and have fun with this." As I walked out of the Changing Room, Ruth, who was talking to the others nearby, looked up and down at me, smiled a very large smile and said, "Hi, Kim. I love your hair!"

Giggling, she walked off. I thought, "Lucky guess," and I continued on. Each person I met said, "Hi, Kim" and gave me a big smile!

Then I heard this, "They know you by your spirit, not by what's on the outside."

You see, it doesn't matter how we look on the outside, if we're tall or short, white, black or brown, in Heaven they know us by our spirits—but they'll still play along with our games. They also don't know us by what sins we had committed while on the earth, all of those have been erased.

Note that Halloween costumes are a counterfeit of this Changing Room. Paul said, "The coming of the lawless one will be in accordance with how Satan works. He will use all sorts of displays of power through signs and wonders that serve the lie." (2 Thessalonians 2:9 NIV)

2011

You'll Never Ride Alone

While praying, I was in the spirit realm as a teenager and saw my white horse, Peal. His back is about six feet high and he has huge hoofs and a long, thick, soft, white mane and tail. He has strong muscles and must be a total of at least eight feet tall. He knelt down so I could get on.

Jesus, who I knew was there, said, "You'll never ride alone."

I looked and as far as I could see, there were many other horses with and without riders. The riders were practicing their riding skills.

Jesus said, "The Army of God is forming. It is not a struggle for God to create such a strong being (referring to my horse). It's not a struggle for Him to make it powerful. The horse has no power in itself, but is just the carrier of the messenger. Likewise, your flesh has no power in itself—it's just the carrier of the messenger."

Translated to Los Angeles, California

I was worshiping Jesus at 7:28 a.m. one day when I was translated to another place. I felt Jesus take my hand, and instantly we were in a coffee shop in Los Angeles. There was a long counter-like bar on the left side of the room and we were standing near a large, round table in the middle of the room where most of the people sat. I began to share the Gospel with them, about Jesus dying for them and how they don't have to be sad, depressed, or hurt because Jesus paid the price for them. I told them how much He loves them.

Then I sat down in a chair and asked if they wanted to accept Jesus—and about five people prayed with me to receive Jesus into their lives! When I stood up, I felt myself leave that room and come back to my own prayer room and then back into my body. I still had the joy and excitement stirring inside of me from praying with the people in the coffee shop to accept Jesus Christ as their Lord and Savior.

Translated to Hawaii

This night while praying, I was almost instantly in Hawaii walking on the beach. I saw a little dark-haired boy throwing shells or rocks into the sea. I walked up next to him, squatted down, and said, "Hi, what are you doing?" He said, "Nothing. My mom and dad are getting a divorce, and they're fighting about where I'll live."

I heard the Lord tell me to say to him, "God has a best friend for you that will be your friend forever. When you grow up, you and your dad will live in the same town and be best friends. You will go to games and watch sports together."

After telling the boy this, he said, "That would be nice because now I only see him when he comes home and kisses me while I'm asleep, because he is working all the time."

We talked awhile before his mom saw us. She seemed concerned about who he was talking to on the beach. She called to him and as he ran to her, he waved bye and said, "Thanks! I feel better now."

I heard him say to his mom, "Hey, that person said everything will be okay," and his mom smiled and waved to me.

Jesus appeared to me on that beach and said, "See, sometimes the things you do aren't great and big, but they are needed." Instantly we were at a waterfall and walked across it. Looking out over the ocean, I could smell flowers and hear birds. We stayed and watched the sun set.

Snowy Mountain

During prayer, Jesus took me to a high snowy mountain and asked me what I saw. I replied, "I see white: peaceful, pure, clean, and refreshing whiteness!"

Jesus said, "There's coming a refreshing, a good, exciting change." He began to clap and dance, saying, "You're going to love it!" I could feel fresh, pure, clean, snow fall on me!

Then we were sitting in front of a wide and thick rock fireplace with a hot fire. I sat in a big comfy chair and cuddled up. Jesus sat across from me. There was soft snow heavily falling outside and piling up on the ground.

I thought, "Aaaah, there is no way that someone could come and disturb us. The snow was too deep for any four-wheeler or hiker to get through!"

Jesus said, "This is our new meeting place, how do you like it?" I thought, "I love it; it's so peaceful and quiet. I love that I don't have to do anything to impress Him. I don't have to dance, clap, sing, or have a clean room. I can just sit and watch the warm fire with Him."

He smiled at me with such love in His eyes at my discovery. He knew just what I was thinking without saying anything.

2012–2014

They Pray for You!

During my worship time, Jesus was holding my face in His hands and saying, "I accepted you even when you were far away from Me. Now you need to accept who you are!"

Then I saw a crowd of people in Heaven, bowing down and praying for me.

Jesus said, "You think you don't have anyone praying for you, but they never stop! They have prayed for you since you were sent, that you'd never quit and never fail to fulfill your destiny. They pray 24-7 and will not quit until you come home. They have prayed for you during *every* stage you've gone through."

Romans 8:34 KJV says concerning Jesus, "Who is even at the right hand of God, who also maketh intercession for us."

Britain

Jesus took me to Britain and into the Flower Room (that's what I call it) in the Royal Palace. There was a cleaning lady who seemed very sad. I watched her while she was leaning on a big table. She would cry, then polish the table, stop, and cry again.

I asked her, "Why are you crying?"

She said, "I will never have anything nice like this."

I took her by the hand and began, in the spirit realm, walking up a set of stairs. She asked, "Where are we going?"

I told her, "To your mansion."

She stopped as though she was scared and said, "Oh no, I'm not worthy to have that!"

I told her, "Because you accepted Jesus in your heart as a little girl, you were made worthy." She nodded, remembering asking Jesus into her life.

Still in the spirit realm, we walked into her kitchen where there was a huge refrigerator. She opened the refrigerator door, looked at all the food, and was so happy.

She said, "This is all mine?" Looking around the kitchen and the other rooms in her mansion. She was so happy and kept saying, "This is mine!" as she ran her hand across the woodwork of many tables and door frames.

We came back to earth and she began to twirl and dance and hop, and dance some more, saying, "I have my own place, I have my own place! Thank you for showing me!" She danced through the door, twirling her dust rag and singing, "I have my own place, I have my own place!"

I stepped back into my world, knowing someone was happy in Britain!

Table in Heaven

Daddy God showed me a table in Heaven with people sitting around it, talking.

I heard them say, "If they serve Him, if they believe in Him, pray to Him, ask Him, or even fight against Him, it doesn't change who He is! He is goodness and mercy! The Kingdom of Heaven is life, and giving, and always changing. The Kingdom of Heaven is advancing, growing, and full of life—it's not stagnant!" It was as if the people sitting at the table couldn't see me, but I could see and hear them.

Daddy God said, "My healing doesn't depend on what people think of Me. Whether they know who I am, or whether they believe in Me, it doesn't change Who I am. I am Goodness, and what they think or do, does not change My Goodness!"

They Want to Teach You, People in White

I was swinging (as an adult) in a garden filled with bright flowers, with Jesus pushing me. Then I was with a minister, named Kathryn Kuhlman, and we talked. She showed me the kids Jesus promised her, they were all around her. They were of all ages and nationalities and so full of love for her.

A bunch of maybe 50 people, dressed in white, came running up toward me. I sensed they were people with giftings, but no relatives to whom they could pass them.

Kathryn said, "They want you to go farther with their anointing than they did." I felt like they wanted me to learn how to trust Jesus, yield to Him more, and learn to move in the supernatural, operating with angels.

White Round Light

Jesus gave me a big, white, round light and I put it in my head! I'm not sure why, but it felt like that's what I was supposed to do with it.

Then Daddy God said, "Follow the eyes of your heart, follow the ears of your heart—not what you see or what you hear in the natural—but the compassion you see and hear from your heart."

Conclusion

I believe everyone who is born again can go to Heaven, and see and play with Jesus without having to die first. Yes, you can actually go see Jesus, the Holy Spirit, and Daddy God.

It's time to live for eternity.

The Father desires for you to draw near to Him and to know Him; to seek Him and Jesus. Father God says you *can* find Him, but you have to want to. You must come away from the noise in the world, quiet the noise in your mind, and seek Him with all your heart.

You can draw near just like Psalm 73:28 says:

> But as for me, it is good for me to draw near to God; I have made the Lord God my refuge and placed my trust in Him, That I may tell of all Your works.

And you can find Him just like Jeremiah 29:13 says:

> Then [with a deep longing] you will seek Me and require Me [as a vital necessity] and [you will] find Me when you search for Me with all your heart.

I believe everyone has a sense of eternity inside them, as Ecclesiastes 3:11 says:

> He has made everything beautiful and appropriate in its time. He has also planted eternity [a sense of divine purpose] in the human heart [a mysterious longing which nothing under the sun can satisfy, except God]—yet man cannot find out (comprehend, grasp) what God has done (His overall plan) from the beginning to the end.

You can know Jesus, and you can know the Father also, but you must seek a relationship with the Father to know Him. John 17:3 says:

> Now this is eternal life: that they may know You, the only true [supreme and sovereign] God, and [in the same manner know] Jesus [as the] Christ whom You have sent.

If you have made Jesus the Lord of your life, then Jesus says we are already in Him and He is in us. And He is in the Father, so wouldn't it be natural for us to hear and see what the Father is doing—since we are that close to Him? It shouldn't be strange that we see and hear our Father. Doesn't Jesus say in John 14:20, "I am in the Father and you are in me and I am in you"?

We need to learn how to trust in the relationship. This is a time of great healing of the heart, great revelation of His amazing love for us, great deliverance from unbelief, and great deliverance from believing lies. And it's all so that the power of God will not be hindered by our wounded souls.

Intimacy can only be found when we slow down, and come away from the noise, put the cat out, turn off the phones, and then both *talk* to the Father and *listen* to what the Father is saying.

Conclusion

If you find it hard to relate to the Father, or Jesus, or even the Holy Spirit who is sent to counsel you and point you to Jesus, then allow Daddy God to heal your wounded soul (mind, will, and emotions) by spending some time talking with Him. A healed soul will allow your heart to open, and you will begin a wonderful journey of fun, intense laughter, and love that fills every part of you.

All of this is only found in His presence.

Remember that stepping over into God's realm is easy. Everything about Daddy God is easy. Entering into His presence is easier than you think. Jesus died for you so you are already righteous enough to enter in. Stepping into the Spirit realm makes any worry or discouragement you may have fall away because you're entering an atmosphere of joy, love, peace, and acceptance—it fills the air!

Begin to relax and enjoy being with the One who thinks about you all the time, and longs to see you every day. Know that He wants to spend time with you, and that He especially wants to play with you!

Mrs. Kim Robinson
Email: Brightlights-kim@att.net

Heaven is Real and Fun

Conclusion

Printed in Great Britain
by Amazon